Double Standards:
International Criminal Law
and the West

Wolfgang Kaleck

2015
Torkel Opsahl Academic EPublisher
Brussels

ISBN 978-82-93081-67-8 (print) and 978-82-93081-83-8 (e-book)

FOREWORD

The promise: real universal justice can contribute to overcoming international crimes and healing the traumas of individuals and of societies. As a lawyer and human rights activist who has been active in pushing for accountability of those responsible for international crimes on behalf of survivors from many regions of the world, I am also aware of the restrictions of (international) criminal justice. In many cases, however, national and international prosecutions for international crimes can indeed constitute an important part of accountability efforts which allow societies to come to terms with past atrocities. If this is the case or not will depend to a large extent on the needs of the affected communities and whether the respective criminal justice mechanisms function in a way that adequately addresses their grievances. But it will also crucially depend on the legitimacy the respective criminal proceedings enjoy in the affected societies.

The project of international criminal justice has, however, increasingly been the subject of criticisms of bias and political selectivity. Although Western states like to portray themselves as global champions of human rights and universal justice, to date, hardly any of those most responsible for torture at Guantánamo, the ill-treatment of detainees in Iraq or war crimes in Afghanistan, Colombia or Gaza have faced trial. The International Criminal Court ('ICC'), which embodies the promise of universal justice irrespective of a perpetrator's office, race, nationality or political weight, has so far only initiated trials against African defendants. International criminal justice purports to be universal, but in reality it often operates – both before international criminal tribunals and at the national level – in a politically selective manner where charges are mostly saved for rank and file soldiers, powerless former generals or leaders who can be brought to justice at low political cost. Scepticism has especially been mounting in the Global South where impunity for the massive human rights violations committed by Western colonial powers has been rife for more than half a century. Repeatedly, international criminal law has been portrayed as a tool of Western domination whose claim to universality is nothing more than an empty ideological superstructure. These criticisms threaten to undermine the legitimacy of international criminal law and they thereby adversely affect its potential to contribute positively to the collective coming to terms with international crimes.

Although much of this criticism is justified, I continue to believe that an international criminal justice system which is based on the idea that even the most powerful are equal before the law and will be held accountable for crimes they committed has the potential to make a difference to the lives of the victims of international crimes, the affected societies and the world. The very claim to universality and the peculiar workings of legal systems open up space to expose existing double standards as contradictory and unjust and to push for accountability of the powerful.

In this book I assess the existing double standards in the application of international criminal law, especially in connection with the question of accountability for international crimes committed by Western states. Its aim is constructive in nature. So far this important debate has been left mostly to the opponents of international criminal law, to the Saddam Husseins and Slobodan Miloševićs who have skillfully relied on the charge of political bias in order to challenge the legitimacy of the courts in front of which they had to defend themselves. In a similar vein, criticisms of the African focus of the ICC and of the universal jurisdiction practice in European countries such as Belgium and Spain have often been deployed by members of African elites whose concerns seem to be mainly driven by the urge to avoid ending up in the dock in The Hague themselves. I therefore consider it crucial that the proponents of a truly universal international criminal law engage with this debate, if what has been one of the most progressive legal developments of the last decades is not to ultimately fail for lack of legitimacy and global endorsement. This book – originally written and published in German in 2012 and now translated and updated – aims to contribute to this discussion.

One motive behind the book is to raise awareness in respect of existing double standards and problems of selectivity amongst practitioners and scholars of international criminal law. Quite often we may lose sight of the fact that a Donald Rumsfeld and a chief executive officer of a transnational corporation can be as much a war criminal as a Muammar Gaddafi or a Joseph Kony, and that the massacres caused by missiles and airstrikes can be just as abhorrent as those perpetrated by the use of machetes and AK-47s.

But even those who argue in principle that Western perpetrators should also be brought to justice may frequently be of the opinion that pursuing their prosecution would not be politically feasible and that the ensuing backlash would undermine the fledgling project of international criminal justice. In my view, however, the aims of further developing the international criminal justice system and of eliminating existing double standards are far from mutually exclusive. Rather, the issue of double standards will have to be discussed and addressed, if the lack of legitimacy, already mentioned, is not to further hamper the development of international criminal law. This book is therefore also a manifesto to not let the practice of international criminal law be restrained by anticipatory obedience and considerations of *Realpolitik*, but to aim for universal justice that truly deserves its name.

As Secretary-General of the Berlin-based European Center for Constitutional and Human Rights ('ECCHR'), a non-governmental organisation that co-operates with human rights defenders from all over the world in order to hold accountable those responsible for grave human rights violations, I am convinced that human rights organizations and survivors of human rights violations themselves have a fundamental role to play in advocating and pushing for the gradual and progressive reduction of existing double standards in international criminal law. In this book I also tell some of their stories and appraise their contributions to the fight against impunity for international crimes. I hope that this narrative will play its part in motivating those who continue to seek justice for grave human rights violations to continue their struggles.

For their comments and suggestions I thank Jörg Arnold, Bill Bowring, Andrea D. Bührmann, Andreas Fischer-Lescano, Anna von Gall, Florian Jeßberger, Albert Koncsek, Andreas Schüller, Alexa Stiller as well as Lena Luczak and Susanne Schüssler from the publishers Klaus Wagenbach. I would also like to thank Jen Robinson and the Bertha Foundation for their support. For their support with the English version I would like to thank Lisa Bausch and Simon Rau, Fiona Nelson, Lindy Divarci and Birgit Kolboske for the translation and the editors from the Torkel Opsahl Academic EPublisher, especially Morten Bergsmo and Gareth Richards.

Wolfgang Kaleck, April 2015

TABLE OF CONTENTS

1

Introduction: International Criminal Law Between Law and Politics[*]

"Winners are never tried for war crimes".

"If you look at the history of war crimes there isn't one instance where a winner of a war has been tried before a Tribunal". This was the claim of Sri Lanka's permanent representative to the United Nations ('UN'), Palitha Kohona, in an interview in the summer of 2009. His country's army is responsible for the deaths of around 40,000 civilians as well as thousands of cases of torture and rape committed during and after the war against the Tamil liberation movement, a conflict that came to an end in May 2009 after 30 years of brutally conducted hostilities on both sides. When asked about legal consequences for crimes committed by the state, Kohona replied that war crimes tribunals have "always been set up for losers. And if you were to take winners then the start would have to be taken elsewhere. Sri Lanka did not drop atom bombs or destroy entire cities during the war".[1]

It is clear that today, around 70 years after the nuclear bombs were dropped on Hiroshima and Nagasaki, Western powers are not the only ones seeking to benefit from the privilege of victors' immunity. It is clear, too, that the debate around prosecuting grave human rights violations is still dominated by arguments grounded firmly in *Realpolitik*.

Even if international criminal prosecutors do take action, for example when the International Criminal Court ('ICC') in The Hague issued an arrest warrant against Libya's former leader Muammar Gaddafi in June 2011, a heated legal debate often ensues. Some of those who objected to the Gaddafi case pointed out that it is only North Atlantic Treay Organisation's ('NATO') opponents – Gaddafi, Milošević or African nationals – who are brought before international tribunals. Others took a different

---

[*] This book was written in German in 2011 for the Wagenbach Publishing House and the German Center for Political Education (Bundeszentrale für Politische Bildung). It has been translated and updated for this edition.

[1] Interview with Palitha Kohona in the *Daily Mirror*, 20 August 2009.

view, advocating confidence in the ICC. They argued that while ideally prosecutions should also be pursued in cases of systematic torture of prisoners and suspected terrorists by the USA and its allies following 11 September 2001, this is not yet possible. The relatively new Court in The Hague needs some time, they contended, to establish itself in an international landscape dominated by Western powers. They argued that the pursuit of dictators such as Gaddafi, while politically motivated, will ultimately pave the way for a practice of truly universal criminal prosecution in the future.

The modern history of international criminal law began auspiciously with the Nuremberg trials in the aftermath of the Second World War. For political reasons, the agenda of universally prosecuting those responsible for the most severe crimes – promised by these trials – was never completed. The progressive development of international criminal justice ground to a halt during the Cold War, when Western powers – despite newly formulated human rights principles and norms – were responsible for a series of international crimes in the course of the suppression of anticolonial liberation movements around the world. Meanwhile, human rights violations were also being committed on a massive scale by Stalin and his successors. During the 1970s and 1980s, courts in Athens, Lisbon and Buenos Aires presided over a number of significant criminal trials relating to the crimes of toppled regimes, but these cases failed to attract much global attention. The 1990s saw something of a revival of the development of international criminal law at the international level, with great optimism around the establishment of the tribunals for ex-Yugoslavia and Rwanda as well as the setting up of the ICC. Today, over 10 years since the ICC came into being and 17 years since investigations were initiated before a Spanish magistrate in the Pinochet case, the international criminal justice system is being criticized on various grounds and has become the subject of great scepticism.

It is true that the practice of international criminal law often leaves a lot to be desired. A great gulf exists between what it promises and what actually occurs. In practice, only a small number of the world's dictators and torturers have to fear prosecution by courts in The Hague or elsewhere. This book focuses on one of the biggest weaknesses of international criminal law: that the law is applied selectively and is predominantly wielded against weak, fallen and toppled autocrats and military leaders. But it also tells the stories of social movements and lawyers to ensure that human rights violators from powerful nations are held to the same standards as those from weaker states.[2]

To date, all suspects brought before the ICC in The Hague, in operation since July 2002, have been from Africa. This is despite the fact that human rights violations have occurred in many other parts of the world during this period. Granted, some of the violations occurring outside Africa do fall outside the remit of the ICC, as they were committed in states that have not signed up to the Court's jurisdiction. But why, for example, was the UN Security Council so quick to give the ICC prosecutor the power to commence investigations into Gaddafi's government in February 2011, while back in early 2009 there was no such resolution passed in relation to Israel's war in Gaza, nor in relation to the war crimes committed by the Sri Lankan government against the Tamil population, nor in the case of the Iranian dictatorship's repression of oppositionists after the elections? Similarly, when such crimes could have been prosecuted in other forums, that is, in national courts, very little action was taken. Prosecutors in Western Europe with jurisdiction over some of these international crimes have pursued mainly African and Nazi criminals along with a few suspects from the former Yugoslavia. Over the past 17 years, following the start of criminal proceedings against the former Chilean dictator Augusto Pinochet and the former Argentine junta leader Jorge Videla, human rights organizations have started to make use of international criminal law, assisting with and initiating legal proceedings in a variety of cases. These efforts were aimed at securing the prosecution of, among others, members of the Bush administration and the US military, the Israeli military and individuals from Russia and China who are suspected of committing international crimes. Yet most of these attempts were thwarted early on by the various prosecuting authorities involved.

---

[2] This aspect is influenced by my experiences as a lawyer and activist. Along with the German criminal complaints mentioned in this book, which concern crimes during the Argentine dictatorships, in Uzbekistan, Guantánamo and Abu Ghraib, I was and am involved in work on behalf of the victims in the following cases: the Mercedes-Benz and Ledesma sugar cases in Argentina which concern these companies' involvement in dictatorship crimes; the Nestlé case in respect of the murder of a Colombian trade unionist; an Austrian criminal case with regard to torture sponsored by the head of the Chechen Republic, Ramzan Kadyrov; criminal investigations with regard to Guantánamo in France and Spain; cases relating to CIA secret prisons in Poland; to the torture of prisoners by UK forces in Iraq; as well as cases in Germany on the Chilean Colonia Dignidad; the CIA abduction of Khaled El-Masri; and the 1999 NATO airstrike on Varvarin.

From a legal and human rights perspective, it is fair to say that the defendants brought before various international tribunals and national courts over the last 20 years were generally not the 'wrong' people. Almost any independent observer would agree that international crimes were committed in the former Yugoslavia, Rwanda, Sudan and the Democratic Republic of the Congo ('DR Congo'), and that the role of the suspects brought before the courts in their commission warranted criminal investigations. The question, though, is why criminal cases were launched *only* in these cases, and *only* against these particular suspects, and why so few convictions have been secured in general.

To answer these questions one could look to political theorists such as Carl Schmitt and the realist Hans Morgenthau, who take a cynical view of the politics of power, emphasizing the primacy of political and *Realpolitik* factors in the sphere of international relations, and considering law as playing only a secondary role. Yet the post-war expansion of the reach and significance of the law on an international level, and the development of international criminal law, would suggest that the *Realpolitik* position, in its pure form, is somewhat outdated. The French lawyer Pierre Hazan has pointed out that international politics has moved from the negative anthropology of realism to the evangelical optimism of liberalism.[3] Yet remnants of the realist theory remain at play, as when powerful states attempt to justify the non-application of international criminal law in certain cases. A classic example is the position set out by former US Secretary of State Henry Kissinger, who is himself suspected of involvement in international crimes, including war crimes in Vietnam and Cambodia. Writing on universal jurisdiction over international crimes, he claims that throughout history the "dictatorship of the virtuous" has often led to inquisitions and witch-hunts, and warns of the danger of "substituting the tyranny of judges for that of governments".[4] While this theoretical debate is not the main focus of this book, determining the relationship between

---

[3]   Pierre Hazan, "Das neue Mantra der Gerechtigkeit", in *Der Überblick*, 2007, vol. 43, nos. 1–2, p. 10. Hazan echoes the words of Ariel Colonomos in his book, *Moralizing International Relations: Called to Account*, Palgrave Macmillan, London, 2008, p. 45, where he writes that "liberalism's congenital evangelism [...] gained ascendency over the negative anthropology of realism".

[4]   Henry Kissinger, "The Pitfalls of Universal Jurisdiction", in *Foreign Affairs*, July/August 2001, vol. 80, p. 86.

law and politics is an important element that will be addressed in each chapter in respect of the analyzed concrete constellations.

1.1. Principles of International Criminal Law

The basic premise of international criminal law is the idea that crimes of a certain magnitude affect humanity as a whole which is therefore obliged to prevent such crimes and punish offenders, particularly if these crimes are not being adequately addressed in the countries in which they were planned and carried out.

International criminal law is set down in international and national statutes and regulates the criminal liability of individuals.[5] It represents a mixture of public international law, which has traditionally regulated relations between states, and domestic criminal law, which is concerned with criminal charges levelled against individuals. The elements of the crimes anchored in international criminal law are based on customary law – that is, on a shared legal practice followed by states on the assumption that this is required by international law – and on international treaties such as the Geneva Conventions, the Genocide Convention and the Convention against Torture. These treaties place states under an obligation to undertake domestic prosecutions against individuals suspected of war crimes, genocide and torture. To facilitate the prosecution of the main offenders from Nazi Germany and from Japan, the Allied powers, when setting up the Nuremberg and Tokyo trials after the Second World War, set out the criteria of a number of crimes that would allow for the establishment of the liability of individual actors as opposed to the liability of the states in whose name they had acted.

In international criminal law, the main criminal offences are known as the *core international crimes* and are set out in the statutes of various international tribunals. The core crimes are: war crimes (serious violations of international humanitarian law which forbids certain methods of warfare), crimes against humanity (murder, torture, rape and other acts carried out as part of a widespread or systematic attack against a civilian population), and genocide (which, according to the traditional and highly disputed definition, includes a range of violent acts, if committed against a national, ethnic, racial or religious group with the intention to destroy

---

5   See Gerhard Werle, *Völkerstrafrecht*, Mohr Siebeck, Tübingen, 2007.

that group). While crimes of aggression – that is, offensive wars in violation of international law – are criminalized in certain circumstances under the Statute of the ICC, the Court cannot currently prosecute such crimes.

The current system provides for domestic courts to play a crucial role in the prosecution of human rights violations, particularly the courts of the state in which the crimes were committed or of the home state of the suspected perpetrators. As such, it is national courts that initially have jurisdiction in such cases. Past experience shows that prosecutions for international crimes are more likely to be pursued by domestic courts where there has been an abrupt regime change, and are less likely in the wake of a more gradual handover of power. In both situations, those eligible for prosecution tend to be members of the current or former elite and, as a result, legal proceedings against them are often averted for political reasons. In such cases, the ICC and courts in other states are entitled to exercise complementary jurisdiction as a kind of back-up system to ensure that perpetrators do not enjoy impunity.

Crimes against international law are often dealt with by courts of an international character: the International Military Tribunal at Nuremberg, the UN criminal tribunals for the former Yugoslavia and for Rwanda, or the ICC in The Hague.

There have also been a number of hybrid courts set up since the mid-1990s to address situations in Cambodia, Sierra Leone, East Timor and Lebanon. These combine certain elements of international tribunals with those of domestic courts.

To a lesser extent, prosecution for international crimes has also been taken up by domestic courts in third, generally Western states. Domestic courts are entitled to prosecute extraterritorial crimes on the basis of the principle of active or passive personality (if the perpetrator or victim is a national of the state in which the court is based) or on the basis of the territorial principle (when the crimes committed affect the state's territory). Crimes can also be prosecuted by domestic courts in the absence of any personal or territorial link between the crimes committed and the state in which the court is based on the basis of universal jurisdiction, as relied on by the courts in Spain and the United Kingdom in the Pinochet case.

International criminal law can thus be applied by international, national and hybrid courts. The discussion in this book is therefore not limited to the work of the ICC and the UN tribunals, but looks at the interplay between the various courts and prosecuting authorities engaged in the practice of international criminal law.

1.2. Prosecution: Horizontal and Vertical Selectivity

In any area of law, there is a certain gap between the letter of the law and how that law is applied in practice. However, in the practice of international criminal law, the law is applied so irregularly as to undermine the very legitimacy of the laws and their claims to universal applicability. The premise of this book is that double standards are applied when pursuing prosecutions for grave violations of human rights. In practice, the assessment of whether or not to prosecute crimes against international law is almost always a political decision made in reference to the situation at hand and involving a great amount of both horizontal and vertical selectivity.

Horizontal selectivity is at play when grave crimes are committed in a number of similar situations throughout a given historical period, but only some of these are prosecuted as crimes against international law. As we will see, raising this point often provokes vehement knee-jerk objections.

In the debate on Nazi crimes in West Germany, for instance, great importance was placed on depicting the annihilation of the European Jewish population as an event of historical singularity, thus preventing the drawing of any historical comparisons that might risk relativizing the Holocaust. Researchers in the field of genocide concentrate in particular on the state-organized, intentional destruction of an entire population group. Historian Christian Gerlach, by contrast, suggests the category of 'extreme and violent societies' in order to adequately address the participation of state and non-state actors as well as other forms of violence.[6] These debates on the historical categorization of the discussed crimes should be borne in mind in the following pages when recourse is had to legal definitions, which are not always helpful in the context of academic discussion.

Prosecution for crimes against international law is also prone to *vertical selectivity*, which refers to the decision as to which of the individuals

---

[6] See Christian Gerlach, *Extrem gewalttätige Gesellschaften: Massengewalt im 20. Jahrhundert*, Deutsche Verlags-Anstalt, Munich, 2011, p. 397.

involved in a situation should be singled out for prosecution. Perpetrators of international crimes who hold high-level office often manage to escape prosecution. The focus is often placed instead on lower-ranking soldiers and other less powerful individuals who are selected to serve as scape-goats. Securing these kinds of convictions is a strategy often employed to appease national and international demands for action while avoiding taking politically sensitive action against major perpetrators.

In assessing the practice of international and national courts, a number of dimensions should be taken into account. Being on the winning or losing side in an armed conflict is one such dimension, but the outcome of legal disputes is also influenced by the dichotomies of state versus non-state actors, colonial powers and colonies, great powers and less powerful states, and the North/South divide. At the national level we are used to observing a number of overlapping categories of discrimination, most no-tably those of class, gender and race. The Cameroonian historian Kum'a Ndumbe III points out how Germany and Japan, while officially losing parties in the Second World War, count in practice among the main bene-factors of the war on the international stage. He goes on to argue that those who ultimately lost out were hundreds of millions of voiceless indi-viduals in Africa, Asia, Latin America and the Pacific region, who had nominally been on the side of the winners.[7]

One particularly stark example of this is provided by the roughly 200,000 women from Korea and other East Asian countries who were raped, enslaved and forced into prostitution by the Japanese army during the Second World War. These crimes were not addressed by the Tokyo war crimes Tribunal as Korea did not participate in the proceedings. For decades, these women's cases were ignored in Korea and even more so in Japan, a country which quickly developed into a political and economic powerhouse. While sexualized violence, together with torture and murder, has been a feature of almost all of the historical cases of crimes against humanity addressed by international criminal law, this particular type of violence has been largely ignored by prosecutors.

All of the situations described here warrant comprehensive, trans-disciplinary analysis. The response to human rights violations affects not

---

[7] Kum'a Ndumbe III., "Vorwort", in Rheinisches JournalistInnenbüro/Recherche Interna-tional e.V. (ed.), *"Unsere Opfer zählen nicht": Die Dritte Welt im 2. Weltkrieg*, Assozia-tion A, Berlin/Hamburg, 2005, pp. 9 ff.

only all levels of the society in question but often the wider international community as well. To date, little comprehensive research has been undertaken on the impact of legal interventions. For this and other reasons, this book makes no claims to completeness. Indeed, the sheer number of armed conflicts and grave human rights violations that have occurred since 1945 would make a complete analysis impossible. This book will focus instead on selected crimes committed by the Western Allied states, that is, crimes committed by those who established the court in Nuremberg and with it the modern system of international criminal law. Such an analysis is easier in the context of Western states than it would be in the case of secretive dictatorships, since the former profess to act in accordance with the principles of democracy and the rule of law, generally operate with a greater degree of transparency and are home to established civil society groups. Therefore, they can more easily be reached by a discourse that has recourse to international criminal law as its main point of reference. Some of the crimes examined in this book date back many decades. Studying these crimes is useful in two ways. It helps us to appreciate how far international criminal law has come and it also allows us to better understand the serious reservations surrounding the practice of modern international criminal law held by many in the so-called Global South, where colonial history coupled with more recent interventions have left great scepticism in their wake.

As most of the criminal proceedings dealt with here are lengthy and highly complex, it is too early to adequately assess their long-term impact. The focus of this book lies instead on identifying trends and hazards in the practice of international criminal law and on devising alternatives for challenging the status quo.

2

The Nuremberg and Tokyo Trials and the First Flaws in the System

The judgment handed down at Nuremberg by the International Military Tribunal ('IMT') on 30 September and 1 October 1946 and the 12 subsequent trials held by the Nuremberg Military Tribunal ('NMT') between 1946 and 1949 did more than simply secure the convictions of 171 major war criminals. The judgments established for the first time the idea that anyone involved in the commission of genocide, war crimes and crimes of aggression could expect to be held accountable for their actions, even if they had been acting within a state structure that legitimated such acts. But even during the Nuremberg and Tokyo trials, in the infancy of international criminal law, certain problems were beginning to emerge that would plague this area of law ever after. By the early stages of the Cold War, the first major flaws in the fledgling practice of international law were becoming evident. Senior functionaries managed to avoid prosecution, legal proceedings were shelved for financial and political reasons, and many of those convicted subsequently received amnesties. In post-war Germany and to an even greater degree in post-war Japan, great swathes of the domestic elite avoided prosecution for political reasons and went on to take up prominent positions in politics, business, the military and the judiciary.

2.1. Victor's Justice?

The main criticism levelled at the Nuremberg trials by the defence and subsequently by the German legal community and parts of the wider German public was that the Allies were engaging in victor's justice (*Siegerjustiz*). A number of factors have given rise to this view. Those in the dock and anybody who feared the prospect of ending up on the defendant's bench were naturally concerned with defending their own interests, while some regime diehards were interested in historical revisionism. Many others simply hoped to repress what had happened. Similar reactions can be found throughout the history of international criminal law. In the course of legal proceedings and public debate, the perpetrators and those close to them often do all they can to divert attention from the accusations and undermine the legitimacy of the trial. But not all arguments put forward by the accused are necessarily unfounded. The debate within the Anglo-American legal sphere raised serious questions about the quality of the Nuremberg trials. One example of these concerns was formulated by the Viennese Jewish émigré and Berkeley jurist Hans Kelsen. Kelsen claimed that the trials had the character of a *privilegium odiosum* (a privilege that brings with it cumbersome duties) imposed on the vanquished states by the victors, who had set up a court made up exclusively of members of the victorious states which had been affected by the crimes in question, excluding representatives of both defeated and neutral states.[1]

The objections to the trials related mainly to the mandate of the Allied courts, their basis in law, the nature of the proceedings and the prohibition of retroactive criminalization in connection with certain charges such as the waging of aggressive war. The legal basis of the tribunal and the method of selection of defendants and judges were set out in the London Agreement and the accompanying Charter of the International Military Tribunal concluded on 8 August 1945 by the Allied governments of the Soviet Union, USA, Britain and France. The defendants were all selected from the defeated German side, while the judges were all nationals of the victorious powers. This criticism was countered by the political justice analyst Otto Kirchheimer, a German-born US law professor, who pointed out that in any political trial taking place in the courts of a victorious power, the judges will to some degree be "victors' judges". He went on to argue that having German judges on the bench would not necessarily have been advantageous for the accused at Nuremberg, as these judges would not have been chosen from the ranks of the Nazi party and its sympathizers.[2]

Similar arguments were levelled against the Tokyo trials at the International Military Tribunal for the Far East which oversaw the prosecution of 28 Japanese generals and politicians who, unlike the defendants in Nuremberg, were charged solely with the crime of waging wars of ag-

---

[1] Hans Kelsen, "Will the Judgement in the Nuremberg Trial Constitute a Precedent in International Law?", in *The International Law Quarterly*, 1947, vol. 1, no. 2, pp. 170 ff.

[2] Otto Kirchheimer, *Political Justice: The Use of Legal Procedure for Political Ends*, Princeton University Press, Princeton, NJ, 1961, pp. 332, 335.

gression.[3] Although the tribunal was more international in nature than the court at Nuremberg – the 11 judges included representatives from the four major victorious Allied powers as well as from China, Australia, the Netherlands, India and the Philippines – the charge of victor's justice is maintained until today in respect of these trials. During the course of the proceedings, which lasted from 1946 to 1948, 25 of the accused were sentenced to death or imprisonment, with the vast majority of those imprisoned receiving life sentences. Some 5,700 members of the Japanese military were put on trial during subsequent proceedings held between 1945 and 1951, with additional trials taking place in other East and Southeast Asian countries.

It was argued during the course of both the Nuremberg and the Tokyo trials that the application of certain criminal charges violated the principle of *nulla poena sine lege*, that is, the prohibition of punishment in absence of a legal basis that was in force at the time of the commission of the crime. Questions were raised as to the legality of the charges of "crimes against the peace" (that is, the waging of an aggressive war), membership in a criminal organization and the overall concept of conspiracy. Despite these concerns, there is now almost unanimous agreement among legal experts that the overall construction of the Tribunal, the composition of the court and the proceedings met accepted legal standards. The International Military Tribunal was not an extraordinary court dealing in victor's justice, but instead attempted to act as a proper international criminal court.[4] Proceedings were carried out as fairly as could be expected according to the standards of the time or, to put it in Kirchheimer's words, if assessed with reference to the criterion of the "creative tension of an undetermined outcome", Nuremberg "was not a simulated trial".[5]

---

[3] On the tribunal generally, see Philipp Osten, *Der Tokioter Kriegsverbrecherprozeß und die japanische Rechtswissenschaft*, Berliner Wissenschafts-Verlag, Berlin, 2003.

[4] M. Cherif Bassiouni, "Das 'Vermächtnis von Nürnberg': eine historische Bewertung fünfzig Jahre danach", in Gerd Hankel and Gerhard Stuby (eds.), *Strafgerichte gegen Menschheitsverbrechen: Zum Völkerstrafrecht 50 Jahre nach den Nürnberger Prozessen*, Hamburger Edition, Hamburg, 1995, p. 19.

[5] Kirchheimer, 1961, p. 340, see *supra* note 2 (author's translation).

2.2. The *Tu Quoque* Debate

Throughout the proceedings in Nuremberg and Tokyo and in many of the subsequent trials, the *tu quoque* ("you too") objection – that is, the complaint that the trials targeted only the losing sides of the war, despite the fact that the Allied powers had committed similar crimes – was raised. The *tu quoque* argument was often directed not only at the court in the hope of being acquitted but also towards the wider public and future historians. The aim was less a question of scoring legal points and more about undermining the political legitimacy of the court in general. One such attempt can be seen in the writing of Carl Schmitt, a German lawyer involved in the rise of the Third Reich, who in December 1949 noted in his diary: "There are crimes against and crimes for humanity. The crimes against humanity are committed by Germans. The crimes for humanity are committed against Germans".[6]

The classic and most widely discussed example of a *tu quoque* situation in a criminal context is the trial of Admiral Karl Dönitz as part of the major war criminals proceedings in Nuremberg. Dönitz faced three charges, one of which concerned illegal methods of naval warfare, specifically the practice of using submarines to attack merchant vessels without making any efforts to save the crew and passengers of the sinking ships. Dönitz's defence lawyer Otto Kranzbühler asked the court for permission to hear evidence from US Navy Admiral Chester Nimitz to prove to the court that Nimitz had given orders for similar methods of submarine warfare to be employed in the Far East. In doing so, Kranzbühler was not attempting to put forward the argument that the USA was also guilty of war crimes in order to relativize the crimes and imply that the USA was in no position to put his client on trial. Instead, he wanted to show that in pursuing these methods of warfare, both the US Navy and his client were acting within the boundaries of the law. His intention was to draw on the victor's code of practice as authority to interpret the relevant provisions of the laws of war to secure an acquittal for his client. Kranzbühler's strategy did manage to cause some disquiet among the ranks of the prosecutors and judges in Nuremberg who were worried that the Allies' methods of warfare would come under greater scrutiny, and possibly even be used for propaganda purposes. Francis Biddle, an

---

[6] Carl Schmitt, *Glossarium: Aufzeichnungen der Jahre 1947–1951*, Duncker und Humblot, Berlin, 1991, p. 282 (author's translation).

American judge at the Court, later described in his memoirs why he argued for Kranzbühler's request to be allowed. He recalls being afraid that they would look like fools if they refused "and it later appeared that Nimitz had torpedoed without warning".[7] A different picture emerged from Nimitz's testimony, which revealed that the crew of Japanese merchant ships were generally armed and therefore seen as too dangerous for the US submarine crews to take on board their vessels. These merchant crews were thus treated as combatants and seen as legitimate targets. In marked contrast to the Germans who, under commands issued by Dönitz, failed to make any rescue attempts, Nimitz testified that the US army provided survivors of such attacks with rubber boats and provisions.[8] Ultimately the Court settled on a pragmatic solution, convicting Dönitz on all three counts and sentencing him to 10 years' imprisonment, but without adding any additional prison sentence for the charge relating to submarine warfare. This case is noteworthy on two counts: it shows that raising the *tu quoque* objection can be a legitimate and useful defense strategy, and that it can trigger substantive debate if the objection is dealt with in a rational way by the court and not simply dismissed out of hand.

This argument was later embraced in other cases. As part of their defense in the RuSHA trial (*Rasse- und Siedlungshauptamt* – Race and Settlement Headquarters), case number eight of the Subsequent Nuremberg Trials dealing with the implementation of plans to destroy national groups in German occupied territories, the accused pointed to the fact that millions of Germans were deported and expelled from Poland, Czechoslovakia and Hungary following the war. This, they argued, showed that that practice of resettlement did not constitute a crime.[9] In the *Einsatzgruppen* trial the defence counsel argued that the killing of innocent civilians could not be tried as a war crime since the Allies had also killed non-

---

[7]   Francis Biddle, quoted in YEE Sienho, "The *Tu Quoque* Argument as a Defence to International Crimes, Prosecution or Punishment", in *Chinese Journal of International Law*, 2004, vol. 3, no. 1, p. 107.

[8]   Nicole A. Heise, "Deciding Not to Decide: Nuremberg and the Ambiguous History of the Tu Quoque Defense", in *The Concord Review*, 2007, vol. 18, no. 2, p. 12.

[9]   Alexa Stiller, "Die Volkstumspolitik der SS vor Gericht: Strategien der Anklage und Verteidigung im Nürnberger 'RuSHA Prozess', 1947–1948", in Justizministerium des Landes NRW (ed.), *Leipzig – Nürnberg – Den Haag: Neue Fragestellungen und Forschungen zum Verhältnis von Menschenrechtsverbrechen, justizieller Säuberung und Völkerstrafrecht*, Justizministerium des Landes Nordrhein-Westfalen, Düsseldorf, 2007, p. 77.

combatants in their bombing of German cities.[10] The tribunals were forced to address this argument in its various forms throughout the subsequent trials and rejected it on a number of different grounds. The courts stressed that a law does not become invalid simply because one of the legislators has itself acted in violation of that law.[11]

Since Nuremberg, the *tu quoque* argument has often been used by accused parties on various sides of the political spectrum. Leaders of the Algerian Front de Libération Nationale (FLN) attempted to use this claim in their defence by pointing to atrocities committed by the French.[12] The argument was also addressed – and ultimately rejected – by the UN Tribunal for the former Yugoslavia in its Kupreškić decision. Saddam Hussein voiced similar arguments against the USA when an American-backed tribunal in Baghdad sentenced him to death.

Writing on Slobodan Milošević's defence strategy before the UN Tribunal for the former Yugoslavia in February 2002, international law scholar Martti Koskenniemi points to the wider problem attached to these kinds of trials of prominent political leaders.[13] Milošević accused the Western powers of having destroyed Bosnia-Herzegovina and argued that the charges were brought against him solely to legitimize NATO's bombings of Serbia in the spring of 1999, bombings in respect of which no prosecutions were ever undertaken. Koskenniemi sees the ex-Yugoslavia tribunal as being lodged between the Scylla of impunity and the Charybdis of show trials.[14] On the one hand, the proceedings constituted a kind of show trial, argues Koskenniemi, since they were carried out by the West as a history lesson for the Yugoslavs and the wider world – indeed this was an explicit aim expressed by the architects of the trial. He says that a fair trial, on the other hand, would require allowing the former president to set out his version of the conflict in the Balkans and establish the context of the charges he was facing. Koskenniemi accepts that this approach runs the risk of granting Milošević a double victory. First, his conviction would carry less weight if he succeeded in demonstrating that

---

[10] Kevin Jon Heller, *The Nuremberg Military Tribunals and the Origins of International Criminal Law*, Oxford University Press, Oxford/New York, 2011, p. 297.

[11] *Ibid.*, p. 298.

[12] Kirchheimer, 1961, p. 337, see *supra* note 2.

[13] Martti Koskenniemi, "Between Impunity and Show Trials", in *Max Planck Yearbook of United Nations Law*, 2002, vol. 6, p. 1.

[14] *Ibid.*, p. 19.

he had been tried according to victor's justice, and second, he would be offered a platform to establish his version of the underlying historical events which would even be accompanied by an "aura of iconoclasm". As Koskenniemi sees it, this paradoxical result is something that tribunals of this kind must simply learn to accept.

2.3. The Tokyo Trials

Criticism levelled at the Tokyo trials was focused on the primacy of the American occupation policy, that is, on the dominant role played by the Supreme Commander of the Allied Powers, US General Douglas MacArthur, in setting up the court and prosecution authorities and on the selection of the charges. The heinous crimes committed by the Japanese in East and Southeast Asian countries were not at the forefront of the proceedings. The affected Asian countries were under-represented when it came to the selection of judges, who were, instead, represented by the colonial powers of Britain, France and the Netherlands. It is therefore justified to criticize the fact that the crimes committed during Japan's occupations were not examined in detail as the Western powers wanted to evade questions about their own colonial rule in Asia being raised.[15] In terms of vertical selectivity, it is noteworthy that the Japanese Emperor Hirohito and his family were exempted from any charges, a move that had been negotiated as part of Japan's capitulation. This was one of the reasons why many of Japan's elite and wider public refused to acknowledge the Tokyo trials.[16]

Two further major issues overlooked by the Tokyo proceedings have come to prominence since the early 1990s and are now the subject of civil proceedings: the aforementioned fate of the 200,000 'comfort women' from Korea, China and elsewhere who were forced into sexual slavery, and the medical experimentation on humans and the use of biological weapons by the Japanese army, particularly by Unit 731. This unit conducted experiments on prisoners in Chinese Manchuria, including the removal of organs from living people, and is said to have been responsible for killing up to 3,000 people. The unit also employed biological weapons which reportedly caused the deaths of thousands of Chinese civilians. At the close of the war, the army doctor and head of the unit, Ishii, ordered

---

[15] Osten, 2003, pp. 73 ff., see *supra* note 3.
[16] *Ibid.*, pp. 105 ff.

the killing of all prisoners and witnesses and the destruction of the facilities. He fled to Japan where he was arrested and interrogated by the Americans, but he was never charged. Suspicion remains that the USA granted Ishii Shirō and his colleagues immunity in exchange for information about the biological weapons programme and the results of the experimentation on humans.

An interesting aspect of the Tokyo trials was the 700-page minority opinion by the Indian judge and jurist Radhabinod Pal, who argued for a variety of reasons that all of the accused should be acquitted.[17] Pal, one of a minority of Asian judges on the bench, had close links to the anti-colonial movement in India, which had partially aligned with Japan during the struggle for independence. Pal's minority decision was not released to the public at the time of trial and continued to be withheld from publication in the post-war period. In the decision, Pal drew attention to the fact that there was no prospect of prosecuting as war crimes the Allied powers' aerial bombings, including the Dresden firebombing and the use of the atomic bomb in Hiroshima and Nagasaki. While Pal stressed that, in coming to his decision, he hoped to serve only the law itself, his words have since been interpreted by Japanese nationalists as evidence that the Tokyo trials were merely an exercise in victor's justice aimed at damaging Japan's reputation.

The establishment of the world's first international criminal court to carry out the Nuremberg trials was one of the last joint political decisions made by the Allied powers. It is crucial to keep in mind that crimes of the scale committed by the Nazis had never been witnessed before and at no point was it suggested that the Allies were guilty of similar crimes during the Second World War. As the international law writer, William Schabas, rightly points out, it would have been a distortion of reality if the tribunal at Nuremberg had established "a tribunal for 24 leading Nazis and then a tribunal for 24 leading Americans and later a tribunal for 24 English leaders",[18] and not simply because of the political impossibility of setting up

---

[17] International Military Tribunal for the Far East, *The United States of America and others vs. ARAKI Sadao and others*, Judgment, Dissenting Opinion of Justice Pal, Part 1 (http://www.legal-tools.org/doc/712ef9/); Part 2 (http://www.legal-tools.org/doc/03dc9b/); Part 3 (http://www.legal-tools.org/doc/2a3d21/); Part 4 (http://www.legal-tools.org/doc/2a6ce2/).

[18] Victor Tsilonis, "International Protection of Human Rights and Politics: An Inescapable Reality (Interview with Professor William Schabas)", in *Intellectum*, 2010, vol. 7, pp. 46–60.

such trials. Against this background it should be acknowledged that strong legal and moral criticism was levelled in the UK and the USA – albeit without real consequence – against the British and US air forces' bombing of German cities. No such domestic criticism was voiced in connection with the Russian massacre of Poles in Katyn or the mass rape committed by the Red Army during their liberation march westwards.

Like many of his contemporaries, Kirchheimer measures subsequent developments in the law in light of the precedent set in Nuremberg. "Had the noble purpose of criminalizing crimes against peace succeeded", he wrote in 1961, "the uncertain juridical foundation of the charge would now be overlooked and the enterprise praised as the rock on which the withdrawal of the states' right to conduct aggressive warfare came to rest".[19]

This rather disillusioned assessment lost some of its justification after the establishment of the ICC in The Hague, a court that would never had come into existence had it not been for Nuremberg. The Nuremberg trials marked the first time that individuals were tried and convicted by an independent court on the basis of criminal provisions set out in an international treaty. The Nuremberg charges of the waging of aggressive war, war crimes and crimes against humanity served as a model for the Statute of the ICC. While the scope of the Tribunals in Nuremberg and Tokyo was limited to one specific situation, the proceedings served long after as the only point of reference for proponents of a system of international criminal justice.

2.4. The Subsequent Nuremberg Trials

The Nuremberg trials became a model for later courts in part due to the choice of defendants during the ensuing trials presided over by the NMT. These saw leading figures from the state, military, business and the Nazi party appear as defendants. In a series of 12 criminal proceedings, members of the Nazi state elite from the spheres of industry, law and medicine were tried by the NMT and, in one case, by a French tribunal in Rastatt.

To this day, these successor trials, which aimed to conduct a legal examination of the liability of the National Socialist elites, are exemplary for their vertical balance of defendants. For prosecutor Telford Taylor and

---

[19] Kirchheimer, 1961, p. 324, see *supra* note 2.

his staff, the trials were an attempt to shed light on the structures of the Nazi state beyond individuals and to portray the complex relationship between bureaucratic decision-making processes and individual responsibility in an accurate and legally meaningful way.[20] A fundamental sociopolitical analysis of the Nazi system laid the foundations for these prosecutions. The impact of these trials on the legal world can still be seen today. Of particular importance are the Doctors' Trial of 23 medical practitioners for their involvement in the so-called 'euthanasia' programme, experiments on humans and the murder of prisoners in concentration camps, and the Justice Trial of 16 lawyers and judges from government ministries and special courts. The trials of the industrialists Friedrich Flick, Alfried Krupp von Bohlen und Halbach and their staff, as well as of management at the IG Farben chemical company are still held up as precedents today. The defendants were charged with exploitation of their workforce of forced labourers and concentration camp prisoners and with pillage of foreign property.

Despite this, many commentators see the successor trials as a failure, arguing that the changing political attitude of the USA towards the German elite became evident during the trials, in particular when it came to the enforcement of the sentences. While the original intention had been to hold 20 trials of 200 to 400 defendants with a particularly comprehensive series of proceedings against economic actors – a Nuremberg II – a lack of financial resources and political support meant that ultimately just 12 trials were held with a total of 185 defendants. With the Cold War looming, the emergent anti-communist Joseph McCarthy and others began to denounce the members of the prosecution in Nuremberg. The Germans benefited from the changing political climate. When granted early release in 1950, Fritz ter Meer, one of the accused in the IG Farben trial, noted that the Americans had become a lot friendlier since they had started having problems in Korea (the Korean War had just begun).[21] Generals Adolf Heusinger and Hans Speidel, a brother of Wilhelm Speidel who had been convicted of war crimes and other charges in the Hostages Trial, acted as advisers to the German Chancellor Konrad Adenauer during discussions on the rearming of Germany in 1950. They exerted

---

[20] See Foreword to Kim C. Priemel and Alexa Stiller (eds.), *NMT: Die Nürnberger Militärtribunale zwischen Geschichte, Gerechtigkeit und Rechtsschöpfung*, Hamburger Edition, Hamburg, 2013.

[21] Heller, 2011, p. 6, see *supra* note 10.

pressure on the American representatives, claiming that the idea of Germany as an ally of the USA against the Soviet Union would be a mere illusion if the planned executions of detainees in Landsberg prison were to go ahead.[22] The political pressure soon yielded results: all the convicts in the 1947 Justice Trial, some of whom had received sentences of 20 years' or life imprisonment, had been pardoned by 1950–51 by High Commissioner John McCloy. Death sentences were commuted to prison sentences, with prisoners being released after a few years. In 1958 the last of the prisoners convicted during the Subsequent Nuremberg Trials was released from Landsberg prison. As the Cold War intensified, those who had received milder sentences or escaped conviction were now required to help build a strong, democratic and capitalist West German state to act as a bulwark against the Eastern bloc. A similar development was evident in Japan, where the political climate meant that no successor trials had been held. All those convicted in the initial trials in Japan had been amnestied by 1958.

2.5. Nazi Trials in West Germany

The prosecution of Nazi criminals after the handover of criminal jurisdiction to West German courts is an unhappy chapter in German post-war history.[23] There was a notable lack of comprehensive investigations into and convictions for Nazi crimes. Many members of the West German elite in industry, administration, the military and the judiciary managed to evade prosecution. Lawyers working during the Nazi regime were not prosecuted by the new German courts, despite the precedent set by the Nuremberg trial in 1947. This is particularly scandalous given that tens of thousands of death sentences had been handed down by the pre-war courts. Some 5,266 death sentences were issued by the *Volksgerichtshof* (People's Court) alone during trials which can only be characterized as a mockery of justice. Yet none of the judges responsible was ultimately convicted for these crimes. Euthanasia and the many war crimes committed in the East went similarly unpunished. Having said that, the establishment of the Ludwigsburg Central Office of the State Justice Admini-

---

[22] *Ibid.*, p. 350.

[23] See, *e.g.*, Joachim Perels, *Entsorgung der NS-Herrschaft? Konfliktlinien im Umgang mit dem Hitler-Regime*, Offizin Verlag, Hannover, 2004; Norbert Frei, *Vergangenheitspolitik*, Beck, Munich, 1996; and Jörg Friedrich, *Freispruch für die Nazi-Justiz*, Rowohlt Taschenbuch Verlag, Hamburg, 1983.

strations for the Investigation of National Socialist Crimes in 1958 did lead to the initiation of a larger number of proceedings. In addition, a number of highly committed lawyers such as Fritz Bauer, prosecutor in the Frankfurt Auschwitz trials, made great efforts to pursue criminal proceedings. Yet the judgments handed down by the courts, particularly in relation to different modes of individual criminal responsibility for Nazi crimes, led to some absurd outcomes. There was a blatant discord between the scale of the crimes committed and the sentences handed down; one lead prosecutor described the court's formula as "one death = 10 minutes in prison".[24] Furthermore, those who had perpetrated crimes as "desk-murderers" while working in administrative roles were able to escape punishment on the basis that they themselves had neither committed acts of brutality nor been motivated by cruelty, but had simply been fulfilling their duties. In trials involving clear cases of direct perpetration, judges often held that additional base motives would be required for a conviction. Where such motives were not found the accused would be convicted as mere accessories to the crime and receive reduced sentences.

A tally from 2005 showed that 36,393 investigations involving 172,294 individuals were opened into crimes committed during the Nazi era. Some 16,740 people were charged and just 6,656 of those were convicted, meaning that 160,000 of the proceedings did not result in any punishment.

Despite all the criticism that can be levelled at the trials, they did leave a valuable legacy that extends beyond their importance in the legal sphere. The documentation of the proceedings, including the trials of the major war criminals as well as the subsequent trials, proved helpful as German society began the process of accounting for and coming to terms with the period of Nazi rule. The case files serve as a useful source for generations of historians, although it is important to bear in mind that the logic underpinning criminal proceedings – establishing individual guilt and the truth as it applies to one specific case – is of only limited use when it comes to historical and sociological investigations. The images and accounts that emerged from the Nazi trials prompted much of West German society to reflect for the first time on Germany's Nazi past, a process aided by the work on the Frankfurt Auschwitz trials that has been

---

[24]   Perels, 2004, p. 225, see *supra* note 23, quoting Barbara Just-Dahlmann who worked at the Ludwigsburg Central Office.

done by writers such as Peter Weiss and journalists including Hermann Langbein.

The impact of the Nuremberg trials was felt around the world, thanks in no small part to the chief prosecutor from the USA, Robert H. Jackson. In a much-quoted passage from his opening words at the trial in November 1945, he made a memorable plea for a system of universal criminal justice free of political selectivity:

> And let me make clear that while this law is first applied against German aggressors, the law includes, and if it is to serve a useful purpose it must condemn aggression by any other nations, including those which sit here now in judgment. We are able to do away with domestic tyranny and violence and aggression by those in power against their own people only when we make all men answerable to the law. This trial represents mankind's desperate effort to apply the discipline of the law to statesmen who have used their powers of state to attack the foundations of the world's peace and to commit aggressions against the rights of their neighbors.[25]

Jackson and his prosecution team, including Telford Taylor and Benjamin Ferencz, who relied on Jackson's views in their subsequent criticism of US politics, took the claim to universal justice very seriously. The US government, however, together with the governments of the other Allied powers, was less committed to the idea. Building on the Universal Declaration of Human Rights, attempts were made under the framework of the UN Human Rights Committee to establish binding agreements on civil and political rights as well as economic, social and cultural rights, efforts that were blocked largely by the USA and the Soviet Union. The euphonious but mostly ineffective human rights discourse of those Cold War years was mostly concerned with drawing attention to the human rights violations of the opposing side for political gain.

In 1946 the UN General Assembly passed a resolution stating that the Nuremberg principles as set down in the statute of the Military Tribunal represented recognized norms of international law. Crimes against international law were also defined in the 1948 Genocide Convention and the 1949 Geneva Conventions, but the implementation of these principles

---

[25] Robert H. Jackson, "Opening Statement before the International Military Tribunal", 21 November 1945 (https://www.legal-tools.org/doc/bbc82b/).

remained a distant prospect. No progress was made towards establishing a permanent international criminal court, as had been proposed by the International Law Commission in 1950 and again with some modifications in subsequent years. By the early 1990s the faltering development of the law led some prominent lawyers, even those open to the concept of international criminal law, to conclude that the Nuremberg principles were in danger of being forgotten and that such a fate would, in time, lend credibility to those who denounced the Nuremberg and Tokyo trials as mere instruments of victors' justice.[26]

---

[26] Bassiouni, 1995, p. 28, see *supra* note 4.

3

Impunity for Western Crimes Post-1945.
Part 1: The Colonial Wars

While the long wait for an international criminal court and a robust system of human rights protection hampered Robert H. Jackson's vision of a system of universal justice, a much greater obstacle was provided by events that unfolded in the various colonies of the Allied forces at the end of the Second World War and in subsequent years.

Critiques of international law arising out of post-colonial theories and posited, among others, by the lawyer Antony Anghie and the TWAIL (Third World Approaches to International Law) group, focus on the fact that international law comprises a series of doctrines and principles developed in Europe – based on European history and experiences – that were then imposed on the wider world.[1] Under that original system only the family of nations, that is, the European countries, could be sovereign states as these were the only states regarded as 'civilized' countries, while non-European states were seen as barbaric, backward and uncivilized. It was only through colonialization that international law was universalized. This line of criticism holds that the current North Atlantic imperial mission to 'civilize' the rest of the world uses terms such as development, democratization, human rights and good governance to justify encroachments on the sovereignty of the countries they target under the banner of 'modernization'.

Similar arguments are put forward by Makau Mutua, a Kenyan-born professor at Buffalo Law School, who sees human rights and the attempt to make such rights universal as a "historical continuum" of an ongoing tradition of the West's conceptual and cultural dominance. The underlying cause of this, he argues, is the West's unshakeable tendency to propagate European values by belittling and demonizing non-Europeans and conceptualizing them as "others". As such, he says, the globalization of human rights is in keeping with the historical trend whereby the sup-

---

[1] Antony Anghie, "Die Evolution des Völkerrechts: Koloniale und postkoloniale Realitäten", in *Kritische Justiz*, 2009, vol. 42, no. 1, pp. 49–63, with further references.

posedly morally superior West attempts to "civilize" the rest of the world.[2]

As the Second World War drew to a close, the European colonial powers were faced with a dilemma. In order to defeat Nazi Germany, it was necessary to mobilize the Third World and to access its material and human resources. To secure these resources, anti-racist and egalitarian rhetoric was employed to construct an ideological opposition to National Socialism. By the end of the war, self-confidence was growing among those in the Third World who had taken part in the war effort, giving rise to growing expectations of liberation from colonial rule. This prompted colonially-minded politicians in Britain and France, who feared losing their colonies and political influence, to try to block binding international agreements that emphasized the right to self-determination of peoples or denounced colonialism. Despite these fears, both states were involved in shaping the new post-war system, which included the Universal Declaration of Human Rights of 10 December 1948 and the Geneva Conventions of 12 August 1949. Furthermore, racial discrimination and political persecution soon became a permanent topic at the fledgling United Nations.

Against this background, it is easy to see what prompted the British Colonial Secretary Arthur Creech Jones to write in a confidential circular to the colonies in 1949 that the Universal Declaration of Human Rights could become a "source of embarrassment" with serious consequences for colonial politics.[3] After defeating the German Reich, France and Britain were particularly interested in restoring their own colonial empires by way of an updated, development-based form of colonialism. Their plans were met with intense opposition, particularly since India and Pakistan had already become independent and Ho Chi Minh in Vietnam and Sukarno in Indonesia had also made pronouncements of independence.

As part of the current debate on universal justice, it is useful to look back at the colonial crimes committed by Western powers, particularly in the period following the Nuremberg trials and the signing of the Universal Declaration of Human Rights. The history of these crimes reminds us that

---

[2]   Makau Mutua, "Human Rights in Africa: The Limited Promise of Liberalism", in *African Studies Review*, 2008, vol. 51, no. 1, pp. 17–39.

[3]   Fabian Klose, *Menschenrechte im Schatten kolonialer Gewalt: Die Dekolonisierungskriege in Kenia und Algerien 1945–1962*, Oldenbourg Wissenschaftsverlag, Munich, 2009, pp. 56 ff.

not so long ago, the same Western states that now champion human rights, humanitarian intervention and good governance were committing international crimes with impunity – the same kinds of crimes they now point to in other countries to justify encroaching on their sovereignty and reordering their political systems.

3.1. Contested Decolonization

The struggles for independence in Indochina, Southeast Asia and Africa against the colonial powers of Britain and France as well as Belgium, the Netherlands and Portugal, which began during or shortly after the war, are referred to as contested decolonization.[4] The colonial powers met these independence movements with tactics of counter-insurgency and colonial rule, including the bombing of civilian populations, forced displacement of parts of the population and mass imprisonment and torture. Many of these acts qualified as war crimes; various also constituted crimes against humanity.

That no one was put on trial for these acts was in part due to inadequacies in the law of the post-war period. This is despite the fact that attacks on civilian populations and the abuse and torture of detainees represented a violation of international humanitarian law, at the very latest by the conclusion of the Geneva Conventions in 1949 and the establishment of a minimum standard applicable to all armed conflicts in Article 3 common to the four conventions. Virtually no international court proceedings were ever initiated in relation to these colonial crimes. While it would have been possible to prosecute the widespread killing of civilians and the use of torture in the courts of the colonial powers, no such prosecutions took place. One factor at play here is that many anti-colonial liberation movements were concerned mainly with winning independence and political power. Where efforts were made to draw attention to colonial crimes, it was done more as a method of agitation than a real attempt to secure prosecutions.

By the end of the Second World War, unrest and insurgencies which were beginning to stir in Africa and Asia faced brutal repression by the colonial powers. In 1944, 300 Senegalese *tirailleurs* who had fought for France in the war were massacred by French forces in Thiaroye, Sene-

---

[4]   For more on this, see *ibid.*

gal as they returned home from battle. They had demanded payment of the salaries, settlements and discharge allowances owed to them. In Cameroon, a region that had provided 80,000 soldiers for service in the Allied forces, French soldiers opened fire on a group of protesters in Douala in September 1945, killing up to a hundred of them. Similar events occurred in Morocco, Tunisia and British-occupied Ghana.[5]

A specific kind of warfare with devastating effects for the affected populations was employed in Madagascar, Malaya, Indochina, Algeria and Kenya, but these atrocities have been largely ignored by history. War crimes were a common feature of colonial wars during this period of contested decolonization. The first armed insurgency in Africa during this period took place in Madagascar between 1947 and 1949. Between 15,000 and 20,000 rebels were involved in the uprising which escalated into a brutal war involving mass killings and torture, and entire regions were ravaged by French troops in the course of counter-insurgency operations. In total 89,000 Madagascans lost their lives, many of them refugees who died of hunger or disease.[6] In late November 1946 the French air force bombed the North Vietnamese port town of Haiphong following disagreements about customs duties. Some 6,000 people died in the attack.[7] Over the course of the war in Malaya, which lasted from 1948 to 1960, the British army who fought against the Malayan National Liberation Army engaged in the destruction of entire villages, mass shootings and the widespread use of torture. The Dutch army waged a bloody war in Indonesia from 1945 to 1949 in order to foil Indonesian independence declared on 17 August 1945. Between 80,000 and 100,000 Indonesians lost their lives in the war. British troops also waged war on European soil; in their fight against the Cypriot liberation movement, they engaged in collective punishment of the civilian population as well as systematic torture in internment camps.[8]

---

[5]   *Ibid.*, pp. 73 ff.; and Rheinisches JournalistInnenbüro/Recherche International e.V. (ed.), *"Unsere Opfer zählen nicht": Die Dritte Welt im 2. Weltkrieg*, Assoziation A, Berlin/Hamburg, 2005, pp. 62 ff., 111 ff., 124 ff., 295 ff.

[6]   Klose, 2009, pp. 74 ff, see *supra* note 3.

[7]   *Ibid.*, p. 67.

[8]   *Ibid.*, p. 78.

3.2. The Mau Mau Uprising in Kenya

In the 19th century, the British army pursued a campaign of destruction in Kenya resulting in major depopulation of Kikuyu land. White settlers set up a feudal regime involving elements of forced labour, surveillance and a system of reservations. After the Second World War, a political independence movement emerged. With the involvement of the Land and Freedom Army, the movement turned into an armed struggle that became known as the Mau Mau uprising. Britain responded to the threat by arming 50,000 counter-insurgency troops. After systematic searches of certain neighbourhoods in Nairobi which was seen as the guerillas' main base, 50,000 people were interrogated and 24,000 were interned in camps. British secret service units used these camps for systematic interrogation involving abuse and torture. Jungle areas outside the cities were subjected to indiscriminate bombardments. Millions of Kikuyu were later forcibly resettled into "protected villages". Over the course of the conflict, 167 members of the British army lost their lives along with 1,819 Africans who were on the side of the British, while on the opposing side there were an estimated 20,000 to 100,000 Kikuyu deaths.

3.3. The Algerian War

On 8 May 1945, which marked the end of the Second World War and the day the world was liberated from National Socialism, the bigotry of Western states became all too evident in Algeria. On that very day, the French army responded brutally to the protests against French colonial rule that had broken out in the Algerian towns of Sétif and Guelma following celebrations marking the end of the war. Entire villages were destroyed by bombing and artillery shelling and between 15,000 and 45,000 Algerians were killed within one month. After a five-year period of preparation, the Front de Libération Nationale (FLN) launched their war of liberation against France in 1954 with attacks on gendarmerie stations and the bombing of civilian targets in Algiers. The French army responded with a brutal counter-insurgency policy which, like the British approach in Kenya, was to serve as a notorious example for counter-insurgency operations during the Cold War. Entire regions were razed as villages were bombed and destroyed, and millions of Algerians were forcibly displaced into protected villages. Following initial setbacks, France sent in large numbers of troops, many of whom had served in Indochina; at times up to

400,000 troops were stationed in Algeria. On 7 January 1957 General Jacques Massu, acting under special powers, took over command in the capital city of Algiers with his 10th Parachute Division. The infamous Battle of Algiers ensued, which would later become the subject of a film of the same name by the Italian director Gillo Pontecorvo. Massu made use of secret service tactics to pursue the FLN cadres, who directed their group's bomb attacks and protests from within the old city. Over 24,000 people were interrogated and roughly 3,000 of these died as a consequence of the torture they endured during questioning. Of particular relevance today is the book *La Question* by the French communist and journalist, Henri Alleg, who was subjected to torture at the hands of French elite troops, which involved the technique later known as waterboarding in the context of its use by the CIA. Alleg made a criminal complaint denouncing the torture while on trial for crimes against the state. He was able to provide a detailed description of the locations of and persons involved in his torture, and his injuries had been medically attested. Despite all of this, and the great interest in his case in France after the publication of his subsequently prohibited book, the proceedings concerning his case as well as many other cases of torture were not pursued.

The war crimes committed by members of the French army were never brought before the courts in France due to a number of amnesties granted by the French legislature in 1962 and the following years. There was a clear contradiction at play here since, at around the same time, France adopted statutes on crimes against humanity along with provisions excluding such crimes from the statute of limitations. This point was raised by Jacques Vergès, defence lawyer in the dramatic trial of the former head of the Gestapo in Lyon, Klaus Barbie, in 1987.[9] Barbie had been charged with the deportation of at least 842 Jews from Bordeaux as well as the torture and murder of the resistance member Jean Moulin. Vergès, a French-Vietnamese anti-colonialist activist, had also acted as a defence lawyer for independence fighters in the Algerian war, including Djamila Bouhired who had been tortured and sentenced to death in Algeria and who Vergès would later marry. In these cases, Vergès used a tactic called the 'rupture strategy' whereby he responded to his clients' charges with argumentative counter-attacks that aimed at undermining the legitimacy

---

[9] For a general view of the trial and critique of the identity politics of the prosecution and defence, see Guyora Binder, "Representing Nazism: Advocacy and Identity at the Trial of Klaus Barbie", in *Yale Law Journal*, 1988–1989, vol. 98, pp. 1321 ff.

of the court and the state. During the proceedings against Barbie in Lyon, Vergès called on two prominent lawyers from Congo (then called Zaïre) and Algeria. Together the defence aimed at demonstrating that there were, at best, only minor differences between Barbie's activities as head of the Gestapo and the German repression of the French Resistance, and France's colonial rule in Algeria. They drew further parallels to the system of apartheid and the oppression of the Palestinians. In his closing speech, Vergès told the court that he knew what racism was. He indicated that he had the greatest respect for the suffering of the deported children of Izieu in eastern France because that suffering reminded him of the suffering of the children in Algeria. On 4 July 1987 his client was convicted of crimes against humanity and sentenced to life imprisonment.

Following public admissions by both former generals of the Algerian army, Jacques Massu and Paul Aussaresses, that they had used systematic torture in Algeria, lawyers took renewed action in 2000 to initiate criminal proceedings. These efforts were thwarted by the French amnesty laws. Only Aussaresses was fined with EUR 7,500 along with his dishonourable discharge from the army and the French Legion of Honour for having glorified war crimes.[10] Ongoing disputes between Algeria and France demonstrate that the colonial past of these countries is far from resolved.[11]

These tendencies continue to the present. There have never been serious efforts to investigate colonial crimes before international courts, to punish any of the surviving perpetrators, to sanction the governments involved or to compensate the victims for the ongoing health problems triggered by the crimes. In response, Kum'a Ndumbe III poses a rhetorical question: When has a rich country with power and influence ever excused itself?[12] The West's inaction when it comes to such crimes can also be partly explained by the fact that many of the practices at play during the latter stages of colonialism are still in use in different guises.[13] A further factor is that independence movements and their political leaders mainly resorted to arguments of human rights and the right of self-determination

---

[10] Klose, 2009, p. 3 f., see *supra* note 3.

[11] See Stefan Ulrich, "Terror. Kein Pardon", in *Süddeutsche Zeitung*, 21–22 August 2010.

[12] Kum'a Ndumbe, "Vorwort", in Rheinisches JournalistInnenbüro/Recherche International e.V., 2005, p. 11, see *supra* note 5.

[13] See Moritz Feichtinger and Stephan Malinowski, "Konstruktive Kriege?", in *Geschichte und Gesellschaft*, 2011, vol. 2, pp. 275–305.

of peoples to advance their fight for decolonization and political power. The call for individuals to be held criminally accountable for colonial crimes was not a high priority.

It was not until the 1990s and 2000s that efforts were undertaken by the human rights movement to seek redress in court for human rights violations that occurred long ago, often without the support of the political leaders of those adversely affected. In October 2006 veterans of the Mau Mau uprising lodged a class action suit with a court in London seeking millions in compensation for the torture suffered in British internment camps. While the British government initially argued that the liability for any compensatory payments had passed over to the Republic of Kenya with independence in 1963, the case was ultimately settled out of court in June 2013, with Britain agreeing to pay a total of GBP 19.9 million (EUR 23.4 million) to 5,228 victims.

In the Netherlands, civil proceedings were initiated in 2009 by relatives of victims of the massacre on 9 December 1947 in the Indonesian village of Rawagede where the Netherlands army killed an estimated 431 people. None of the soldiers or officers involved in the massacre had ever been brought before a court. In September 2011 the court of first instance in The Hague decided that the crime at issue was not subject to a statute of limitation and in the following, the case was settled through the payment of compensation and a formal apology by the Dutch state.[14] And the survivors' quest for justice in Dutch courts is still ongoing. In August 2013 ten widows of men who had been summarily executed on the island of Celebes (Sulawesi) obtained a settlement along similar lines. In a further case, the district court of The Hague established in 2015 (in an interlocutory decision) that the Netherlands is liable for damages of the widows and children of victims of summary executions in the former Dutch East Indies.

---

[14] An interesting discussion unfolded on a Dutch web site after the first decision in the case was handed down in September 2011. Under the heading "Open the Flood Gates" commentators noted that if the four claimants in the Rawagede case were to be successful in their claims, there would have to be compensation for the tens of thousands of other victims of the colonial war as well as for the relatives of the 220,000 forced labourers murdered by the Japanese and – according to another commentator – for the victims of human rights violations committed by the Indonesian government in East Timor. See "Rawagede: still waiting for Dutch aid money", RNW Archive, 13 September 2011, available at http://www.rnw.org/archive/rawagede-still-waiting-dutch-aid-money, last accessed on 24 March 2015.

In the summer of 2011 the family of Patrice Lumumba, Congo's first elected president, lodged a criminal complaint with the public prosecutor in Brussels against surviving former members of the Belgian military and ministries suspected of involvement in Lumumba's murder. An investigation was launched by the Federal Prosecutor's Office in December 2012 which, at the time of writing, focuses on eight surviving Belgian suspects.

4

Impunity for Western Crimes Post-1945.
Part 2: The Vietnam War

The counter-insurgency methods tested in Malaya, Kenya and Algeria went on to be used throughout the Cold War, predominantly by the USA and their local allies in Indochina and in Central and South America. During this period, US forces in Indochina were responsible for the most egregious war crimes committed by a Western power since the Second World War. Wars of aggression and protracted carpet bombing operations were undertaken in South and North Vietnam, Laos and Cambodia. US forces were involved in a string of war crimes during this time, including the use of prohibited weapons as well as the killing and rape of civilians, and the widespread torture and killing of prisoners of war suspected of being members of the Viet Cong.

The phase of the conflict known as the Vietnam War began with the entry of a US warship into the Gulf of Tonking in North Vietnam in August 1964 and the subsequent bombing of the area by the US Air Force, and was brought to an end with the ceasefire of 27 January 1973. The deployment of two million tons of bombs and the use of napalm and the defoliant Agent Orange in populated areas violated Articles 22 and 25 of the 1907 Fourth Hague Convention on the War on Land and amounted to grave breaches of the 1949 Fourth Geneva Convention that, according to its Article 147, constitute war crimes which must be investigated and prosecuted by all states parties. US forces were responsible for violating Article 23(a) of the Fourth Hague Convention and the 1925 Geneva Protocol on poisonous gases by spraying 700,000 hectares of land with various chemicals and poisonous gases that caused damage to the health of over 100,000 people.[1] In addition, there was the large-scale resettlement of civilian populations and their internment in 'strategic hamlets' that were controlled by military and police and effectively operated as labour camps. Large numbers of protected structures such as hospitals, churches, schools and dykes were also destroyed. Search and destroy missions using

---

[1] See Heiko Ahlbrecht, *Geschichte der völkerrechtlichen Strafgerichtsbarkeit im 20. Jahrhundert*, Nomos Verlagsgesellschaft, Baden-Baden, 1999, pp. 177 ff.

a combination of aerial bombing and ground troops resulted in the complete destruction of entire villages and tens of thousands of detainees were tortured and killed. As part of the CIA's 1967 countrywide Phoenix Program, persons suspected of being members of the Viet Cong were captured, arrested and often imprisoned in secret camps where they faced interrogation, torture and 'liquidation'. Under the programme, new methods of interrogation that involved psychological torture and the administration of drugs were employed. Relying on publicly available documentation as well as investigations by the US Congress, the historian Alfred McCoy estimates that around 20,000 Viet Cong suspects were subject to extrajudicial execution.[2] The methods of warfare used by US forces during the war, with their millions of victims, are legally classifiable as crimes against humanity. Under the treaties and customary law in force at the time, the actions of the US forces in Vietnam also qualify as war crimes.

4.1. Military Courts and the My Lai Massacre

As international jurisdiction was not an option, US military courts were the only courts with the power to pursue investigations and prosecutions for crimes committed by the US army during the Vietnam War. Between January 1965 and March 1973 military courts convicted a mere 201 members of the US armed forces of crimes against the Vietnamese population. Some 20 of the convictions were for what amounted to war crimes; the other offences were committed by soldiers while off duty. The most prominent of the trials was that of Lieutenant William Calley and Captain Ernest Medina for their roles in the My Lai massacre. The massacre occurred during a counter-insurgency operation by US ground troops on 16 March 1968 in the hamlets of Xom Lang and Binh Thay in the Son My region and resulted in an estimated 504 Vietnamese fatalities, the majority of whom were women, elderly and children; 233 children under the age of 14 were killed in the attack.[3]

---

[2]   Alfred W. McCoy, *Foltern und foltern lassen: 50 Jahre Folterforschung und -praxis von CIA und US-Militär*, Zweitausendeins Verlag, Frankfurt a.M., 2005, pp. 79 ff., 184.

[3]   The massacre was made public largely thanks to news reporting by Seymour Hersh and others as well as complaints made by US soldiers. The publication of photographs by the army photographer Ronald Haeberle also played an important role in the debate on My Lai. The photographs mainly depict frightened individuals, groups of women and children and the corpses. While they do not show the actual killings, together with the numerous

News of the massacre sent shock waves through American society, particularly as accounts by veterans of the war made it increasingly clear that while My Lai might have been the largest instance of the killing of civilians, this kind of incident was a routine occurrence in South Vietnam. The Nixon administration and the US Congress launched reviews into the massacre and other reported incidents, and instructed various government and army departments to carry out investigations. In his survey of these investigations, in particular the commission led by Lieutenant General William Peer, the historian Bernd Greiner describes how genuine investigations were obstructed for a variety of reasons ranging from political intervention to the sympathetic attitude of army investigators.[4] Eleven GIs and 25 officers were charged in connection with the My Lai massacre, but the army commanders in charge opted to have just six cases pursued by the military courts. Despite the existence of solid evidence against them, Oran Henderson, Eugene Koutouc, David Mitchell and Ernest Medina were all acquitted while another, Charles Hutto, was dishonourably discharged. Calley was the only remaining defendant in a trial that attracted great public interest. He was convicted of the murder of 22 Vietnamese civilians and of one count of attempted murder and sentenced to life imprisonment with hard labour. In subsequent proceedings, Calley's sentence was reduced to 20 years and later to 10 years. In 1974 the sentence was lifted due to procedural errors in his trial and Calley was freed.

4.2. The Command Responsibility Debate

The war crimes issue is just one reason why an examination of the legacy of the Vietnam War is relevant to the current discussion. The entire public debate, particularly in relation to the military court proceedings against Calley, is of great interest since unlike the case of French war crimes in Algeria, public pressure in the USA led to official investigations and a small number of courts martial. Other than as part of Viet Cong propaganda, no efforts were made by the Vietnamese side to seek investigatory or other legal proceedings into US crimes. This might be explained in part by the fact that the Viet Cong and the North Vietnam army were also re-

---

eyewitness accounts, the pictures provide a detailed account of the events of 16 March 1968.

[4]   For the full account, see Bernd Greiner, *Krieg ohne Fronten: Die USA in Vietnam*, Hamburger Edition, Hamburg, 2007.

sponsible for numerous war crimes which the Vietnamese government hopes to avoid revisiting.[5] At the time of writing, the economic co-operation between the two countries means that the pursuit of legal action in connection with the crimes committed during the war would be seen by many as inopportune. In the USA, discussion of the case tended to focus on why Calley was the only person brought before and convicted by a court.

The question of criminal responsibility for the crimes proved to be highly controversial. American society, deeply troubled by the events of the Vietnam War and the My Lai massacre trials, entered into a period of intense national debate and self-reflection. Writing in the *New York Review of Books* in March 1971, the renowned author Neil Sheehan wrote:

> We are conditioned as a nation to believe that only our enemies commit war crimes. [...] Do you have to be Hitlerian to be a war criminal? Or can you qualify as a well-intentioned President of the United States? [...] If you credit as factual only a fraction of the information assembled here about what happened in Vietnam, and if you apply the laws of war to American conduct there, then the leaders of the United States for the past six years at least, including the incumbent President, Richard Milhous Nixon, may well be guilty of war crimes.[6]

In the article, Sheehan reviewed 24 recently published books on the war and the war crimes committed by the USA. Sheehan's suggestion that Calley's high-ranking superiors can and should be put on trial was echoed by many legal commentators. In the context of this debate, it is helpful to take a closer look at the legal concept of superior or command responsibility[7] since the relevance of the vertical dimension of the criminal law, that is, the question which persons are chosen to face prosecution in a given case, extends above and beyond the My Lai case.

The problems with the My Lai proceedings began with the choice of accused. The higher-ranking military members were never tried and were never even the subject of investigation despite the fact that the mas-

---

[5]   *Ibid.*, pp. 27, 47, and in particular on the Hue massacre attributed to the Viet Cong, p. 259.

[6]   Neil Sheehan, "Should We Have War Crimes Trials?", in *The New York Times Book Review*, 28 March 1971.

[7]   See Chantal Meloni, *Command Responsibility in International Criminal Law*, Asser Press, The Hague, 2010.

sacre was a result of a systematic military practice. Even the commanding officer of the unit responsible for the massacre, Medina, was acquitted by the court of first instance. This led many lawyers to draw a clear distinction between the My Lai proceedings and the historic verdict of the military tribunal in Tokyo in 1946 in the trial of the commander of the Japanese forces in the Philippines, General Yamashita Tomoyuki , for the extensive litany of war crimes committed by the Japanese army.[8] Yamashita's defence argument that in many cases he was not even present at the scene of the crimes did not satisfy the court and he was sentenced to death for the crimes of his subordinates under the doctrine of command responsibility. Justifying its decision, the tribunal pointed to the prolonged duration of the crimes and stated that it was unnecessary to expressly prove that Yamashita had ordered the crimes in question. According to the tribunal, his criminal liability resulted from the fact that he would or should have known about the crimes and would have been in a position to prevent them.

It follows that, had the US military courts followed this approach in connection with My Lai, many high-ranking military and political figures would have ended up on the defendants' bench.[9] These questions were not just of legal interest; they also became an important part of the political debate on Vietnam. At a rally in New York in April 1971, spokesperson for the Vietnam Veterans against the War and the US Secretary of State at the time of writing, John Kerry, told the crowd:

> We are all of us in this country guilty for having allowed the war to go on. We only want this country to realize that it cannot try a Calley for something which generals and Presidents and our way of life encourage him to do. And if you try him, then at the same time you must try all those generals and Presidents and soldiers who have part of the responsibility. You must in fact try this country.[10]

---

[8]   Ahlbrecht, 1999, pp. 177 ff., see *supra* note 1.

[9]   *Ibid.*, pp. 180 ff.

[10] Quoted in Patrick Hagopian, *The Vietnam War in American Memory: Veterans, Memorials and the Politics of Healing*, University of Massachusetts Press, Amherst, 2011, p. 60.

4.3. The Russell Tribunal

While it was clear for those following the public debate that the USA had committed war crimes in Vietnam, the army proved reluctant to conduct investigations or pursue prosecutions. Pervasive impunity for grave international crimes was a common feature of the post-war period as a whole. Criticism of this trend began to grow, with the Vietnam War sparking protests by groups in the USA and around the world, including by the emergent student movement. In 1967 the mathematician and philosopher Bertrand Russell, together with a number of his peers, began setting up unofficial 'courts of opinion'. The most famous of these was the International Tribunal on the American War Crimes in Vietnam presided over by Jean-Paul Sartre. The court had no legal powers but was intended instead as an alternative response to the ongoing failure of Western states to apply the Nuremberg principles to crimes like the Vietnam War. The aim of the tribunal, according to Sartre, was the "resuscitation of the jus contra bellum which was still-born at Nuremberg – the substitution of ethical and juridical rules for the law of the jungle".[11] The tribunal sat in Stockholm and Roskilde in 1967 and dealt, among other allegations, with charges of waging an illegal war of aggression and violations of international humanitarian law. The tribunal's reports and results were widely published.

The success of the Vietnam tribunal in highlighting the crimes committed during the war prompted a second Russell tribunal that sat from 1974 to 1976 in connection with dictatorships in Latin America. Subsequent Russell tribunals were set up to examine human rights violations in Germany in connection with the counter-terrorist measures taken during the 'German Autumn' of 1978, the genocide of American Indians, and human rights in psychiatry. A further court, the Permanent Peoples' Tribunal in Rome, established by Lelio Basso, focused on illegal acts of aggression such as the Soviet invasion of Afghanistan in 1979 and the US military intervention in Nicaragua in 1984, as well as global problems including decolonization, the right of self-determination of peoples, third world debt and the environment. Various people's courts have also turned their attention to crimes against international law, such as the impunity for crimes against humanity in Latin American and the Armenian genocide.

---

[11] Quoted in John Duffett, (ed.), *Against the Crime of Silence: Proceedings of the International War Crimes Tribunal*, Simon and Schuster, New York, 1968, p. 43.

One such court with significant impact was the Women's International Tribunal on Japanese Military Sexual Slavery held in Tokyo in 2000 to investigate Japanese war crimes during the Asia-Pacific War with a focus on the 200,000 'comfort women' who were subject to sexual slavery at the hands of the Imperial Japanese army in Korea and other countries. The tribunal acted "out of the conviction that the cornerstone of the international and domestic rule of law is legal accountability – the calling to account of individuals and states for policies and activities that grossly violate established norms of international law".[12] For decades, a patriarchal consensus has made it impossible for the victims of sexual slavery to tell their story and receive compensation for the ongoing trauma suffered. Thanks to years of preparation and careful legal work carried out by those involved, the tribunal made a huge contribution to scholarly research on the long-neglected topic of sexualized violence in armed conflict. The feminist legal scholar Sonja Buckel writes of the beginning of the end of the culture of impunity for sexual violence "as the result of a transnational process of norm generation" whereby new standards are gradually implanted within the transnational legal order by a range of different protagonists.[13] The tribunal also proved beneficial to the legal cases taken on behalf of the generally elderly survivors in Japan and South Korea. The women's case was taken up by the government of South Korea. The Japanese government, however, still refuses to make official reparations, recommending instead that the victims should look to private compensatory funds.

These tribunals were established with a variety of aims and for a variety of reasons. One of the main grounds for their work was the prevalence of double standards when it came to prosecuting crimes against international law. These double standards were most obvious in relation to the Vietnam War and the Japanese war crimes against women. In both of these cases, the tribunals managed to draw attention to the respective crimes across a broad spectrum of society, to document the crimes and to

---

[12] Women's International Tribunal on Japanese Military Sexual Slavery, *The Procecutors and the Peoples and the Peoples of the Asia-Pacific Region v. Hirohito Emperor Showa and others*, PT-2000-1-T, Judgement, 4 December 2001, para. 9.

[13] Sonja Buckel, "Feministische Erfolge im Kampf gegen die Straflosigkeit von sexueller Gewalt im Krieg", in Insa Eschebach and Regina Mühlhäuser (eds.), *Krieg und Geschlecht: Sexuelle Gewalt im Krieg und Sex-Zwangsarbeit in NS-Konzentrationslagern*, Metropol, Berlin, 2008, p. 210.

make a valuable contribution to the legal discourse. Subsequent tribunals on ex-Yugoslavia and the Iraq war failed to have such a strong impact, partly because there had already been extensive coverage in the media on the legality of the wars and suspected war crimes committed by NATO, the USA and Britain.

Just as with the human rights issue arising from the wars of colonial liberation, the end of the Vietnam War brought a range of legal proceedings. In 1980 Vietnam veterans lodged a class action against companies including Monsanto and Dow Chemical that had produced Agent Orange. The case was settled in 1984 for a reported sum of USD 180 million in compensation. Despite the large payment, there was dissatisfaction with the settlement in part because the sheer number of claimants meant that victims stood due to receive compensation of just USD 12,000 each.

In January 2004 a Vietnamese group of Agent Orange victims lodged a new suit with the Federal Court in New York against Monsanto and Dow Chemical. Judge Jack B. Weinstein, who also decided on the US veterans' case in 1984, dismissed the claim holding that Agent Orange had not been classified as a chemical weapon under international law at the time of the war, as it was never intended to be used on humans. He also argued that the companies enjoyed the same degree of immunity as the government which was not involved in the case. This decision was affirmed by the US Supreme Court in 2007.

Notwithstanding these mixed results, victims of Agent Orange continue to demand justice: in June 2014 the 73-year-old Tran To Nga, who had been affected by Agent Orange spraying in South Vietnam, sued 26 US companies before the French Superior Court in Évry for producing and supplying the toxic chemical.

5

Yugoslavia, Rwanda and Co.:
The Chequered Legacies of the Tribunals

At the time of the Cold War, crimes against international law could only be taken up, under limited circumstances, before national courts. Right up to the beginning of the 1990s, efforts by the United Nations International Law Commission to establish a permanent international criminal court remained fruitless. That the genocides in ex-Yugoslavia and Rwanda should then be singled out for investigation by international *ad hoc* tribunals cannot be convincingly explained by the established historical narrative. This narrative posits a slow but steady development, aided by the growing significance of the human rights doctrine as promoted by liberal democracies in the West since the Second World War and the proclamation of the Universal Declaration of Human Rights. With the end of the Cold War, any lingering impediments caused by the tension between the blocs fell, clearing the way for the indomitable ascent of human rights.

This portrayal of events is contested by a number of young historians such as Stefan-Ludwig Hoffmann and Samuel Moyn,[1] who see the growth of human rights since the Second World War as a much more fragmented and inconsistent process. They maintain that the main catalyst for the development of human rights was not the Holocaust or the will to prevent future genocides, but the fight for political hegemony. The non-binding and non-enforceable nature of the Universal Declaration of Human Rights and other post-war conceptions left them so open to interpretation that they could be relied upon at will by any party through the vagaries of the language of diplomacy and international relations. At the beginning of the Cold War, the USA and other Western states called the socialist states out on their deficient political and civil rights records. The Soviet Union, in turn, condemned the racial discrimination in southern US states as well as America's disregard for collective economic rights. As we have seen, human rights were not a priority for the anti-colonial inde-

---

[1] See the contributions in Stefan-Ludwig Hoffmann (ed.), *Moralpolitik: Geschichte der Menschenrechte im 20. Jahrhundert*, Wallstein, Göttingen, 2010, and Samuel Moyn, *The Last Utopia: Human Rights in History*, Harvard University Press, Cambridge, MA, 2010.

pendence movements and emergent states, which focused instead on securing independence, the right to self-determination and the right to development. It was not until the late 1970s that the concept of human rights became established as a virtually incontestable political mainstay. The Conference on Security and Co-operation in Europe process and other developments saw the communist bloc beginning to crumble, while in the West alternative political and societal utopias began to lose their allure. According to this version of events, the human rights movement, with its purist moralist approach that completely lacks any genuine political vision of a different society, continued to gather support before ultimately emerging as the last remaining utopia. Similar arguments on the origin of international criminal law are put forward by Frédéric Mégret, who focuses on the correlation between the end of the Cold War and the proclaimed end of history, which for him amounts to the end of politics. He argues that in a world of growing economic and social inequality, the social state as a model for the nation state is in decline while we witness the rise of the penal state instead. This is reflected at a global level in the system of international criminal justice, which he describes as the "acceptable face of globalisation", where questions such on the global distribution of riches are not entertained. By "symbolically prioritising retributive over distributive justice", the adoption of the Statute of the ICC in Rome is, he says, a world away from Porto Alegre, where critics of globalization traditionally convened to seek alternatives to the mainstream economic order.[2]

According to the international law scholar Bernhard Graefrath, the establishment of the tribunals on ex-Yugoslavia and Rwanda can be attributed to the unique political situation presented by these cases; unlike in other armed conflicts, none of the permanent members of the UN Security Council had any involvement in the fighting in either country.[3] This explanation is unconvincing. Apart from the Western crimes already described and grave crimes committed by the Soviet Union, there were three major historical criminal episodes that escaped legal investigation: the

---

[2]   Frédéric Mégret, "Three Dangers for the International Criminal Court: A Critical Look at a Consensual Project", in *Finnish Yearbook of International Law*, 2001, vol. 12, pp. 208 ff.

[3]   Bernhard Graefrath, "Jugoslawien und die internationale Strafgerichtsbarkeit", in Gerd Hankel and Gerhard Stuby (eds.), *Strafgerichte gegen Menschheitsverbrechen: Zum Völkerstrafrecht 50 Jahre nach den Nürnberger Prozessen*, Hamburger Edition, Hamburg, 1995, pp. 295–324.

politically motivated murder of an estimated 500,000 people, mainly communists, by the Indonesian army, police and a coalition of militias in 1965 and 1966;[4] the bloody massacre in former Biafra – now part of Nigeria – in 1971; and the mass violence in what is now Bangladesh from 1971.[5] The Security Council veto powers did not have any more or less of a strategic interest in these places than in ex-Yugoslavia or Rwanda, nor did any other states call for criminal proceedings to be launched against the perpetrators. The inaction in these cases was simply down to a lack of interest coupled with the UN's oft-demonstrated inability to prevent mass murders throughout the 1960s and 1970s. The reaction to these events corroborates of the theory put forward by Hoffmann and Moyn – none of the hegemonic projects pursued by the major powers could hope to benefit from efforts to push for justice in regard of these massive atrocities.

The political interests of Western states also ensured that no international courts were ever tasked with investigating the crimes committed just a few years after or at the same time as the genocides in ex-Yugoslavia and Rwanda by the Indonesian,[6] Haitian, Guatemalan,[7] Philippine[8] and Turkish[9] governments, all of whom are close partners of the West.

---

[4] Christian Gerlach, *Extrem gewalttätige Gesellschaften: Massengewalt im 20. Jahrhundert*, Deutsche Verlags-Anstalt, Munich, 2011, pp. 27 ff.

[5] *Ibid.*, pp. 165 ff. Following the tribunals established for ex-Yugoslavia and Rwanda, a number of other special tribunals have been set up over the past years. These include the Special Court for Sierra Leone, the Khmer Rouge Tribunal in Cambodia, a criminal court in Kosovo, the Special Panel in East Timor and the Special Tribunal for Lebanon. See: International Committee of the Red Cross, "Ad hoc tribunals" (https://www.legal-tools.org/doc/1b2726/); see also Deutscher Bundestag, "Aktueller Begriff: Internationale Strafgerichte" (https://www.legal-tools.org/doc/5bf3e8/).

[6] See Christopher Hitchens, *Die Akte Kissinger*, Deutsche Verlags-Anstalt, Stuttgart, 2001, which, in the chapter on East Timor, examines the role of Henry Kissinger, then Secretary of State, and the weapons supplied to Indonesia by the USA.

[7] On this, see chapter 6.

[8] Between 1971 and 1986 there were widespread reprisals, including extra-judicial killings and torture, against opponents of the Western-sponsored dictator Ferdinand Marcos. Already earlier, communists had been the target of persecution in the Philippines that was supported by the US army.

[9] In the first half of the 1990s the Turkish army, together with special forces and village guards, resorted to ruthless violence against the armed Kurdish independence group, Kurdistan Workers' Party (PKK), and the Kurdish civilian population. Thousands of Kurdish villages were razed and destroyed, hundreds of thousands of people were internally displaced, tens of thousands killed, though it remains unclear how many of these were armed

---

While the discussed explanations might go some way to elucidate the great growth in the prominence of human rights in the early 1990s and why the UN and other international organizations failed to take adequate action in many situations of grave human rights violations, but they do not shed light on the question of why it was the events in ex-Yugoslavia and Rwanda that prompted the establishment of two international tribunals. The explanation for this is likely to lie in the much discussed failure of the international community, the Western powers and the UN to take action to prevent the mass murder that was playing out in these two places in full view of the rest of the world.[10] As such, the establishment of the two tribunals was motivated less by a belief in justice or the hope of preventing future acts of violence and more by the desire to be seen as taking action and to distract from the Western states' previous failure to prevent the slaughter.[11] It seems to be the case that when the tribunals were established in 1993 and 1994, none of the Security Council veto powers expected that the tribunals would pursue their vaguely defined mission with such rigour or that the idea of individual criminal responsibility for crimes against international law would develop much momentum. This appraisal of the situation was confirmed by Madeleine Albright, the former US Secretary of State, in her testimony before the International Criminal Tribunal for the former Yugoslavia ('ICTY') on 17 December 2002. She explained that it had been easy to obtain the agreement of the Security Council in February 1993 since at that point nobody actually believed that the court would ever be able to function. Initially, the tribunals did not have a budget and seemed, even to those working there, to be little more than an insignificant and powerless "Potemkin court".[12]

---

fighters; tens of thousands more were tortured and thousands disappeared. While Turkey has lost hundreds of respective cases before the European Court of Human Rights and was forced to pay millions of euros in compensation, the perpetrators have never had to face criminal proceeding either in Turkey or any other European country.

[10] See the memoirs of the Canadian General Roméo Dallaire, *Shake Hands with the Devil: The Failure of Humanity in Rwanda*, Arrow, London, 2004, and the case brought in the Netherlands by the Mothers of Srebrenica against the Dutch state.

[11] Mégret, 2001, p. 208 f., see *supra* note 2.

[12] See the testimony of Madeleine Albright before the UN tribunal for ex-Yugoslavia on 17 December 2002 in the trial of Biljana Plavšić, available at http://www.icty.org/x/cases/plavsic/trans/en/021217IT.htm, last accessed on 2 April 2015; and Marko Attila Hoare, "Genocide in Bosnia and the Failure of International Justice", p. 6 (https://www.legal-tools.org/doc/56e228/).

5.1. The UN International Criminal Tribunal
for the Former Yugoslavia

Through the adoption of Resolution 827 on 25 May 1993, the UN Security Council decided "to establish an international tribunal" to prosecute "persons responsible for serious violations of international humanitarian law committed in the territory of the former Yugoslavia" since 1 January 1991. Under its statute, which would serve as a blueprint for subsequent tribunals, the ICTY in The Hague has jurisdiction over war crimes, crimes against humanity and genocide. Between its establishment and the last indictments in 2011, the tribunal examined charges against a total of 161 individuals. Some 74 of these proceedings ended with convictions, while 18 of the accused were acquitted. At the time of writing, some 20 proceedings were still ongoing, including the high-profile trials of Radovan Karadžić and Ratko Mladić.

The tribunal, the first international criminal court since Nuremberg, has necessarily been a source of some controversy ever since its establishment in 1993. This is only partly due to the fact that the court was the first of its kind to have to grapple with the complex legal and practical issues attached to international trials in respect of international crimes. Furthermore, the nature of the nationalist conflicts in ex-Yugoslavia entailed that all the Yugoslavian republics made repeated attempts to undermine the court's efforts to prosecute their nationals. The tribunal was mired in further controversy during the NATO war against rump-Yugoslavia when its first chief prosecutor, Canadian Louise Arbour, initiated the issuance of an arrest warrant against the then president Slobodan Milošević. The Serbian elite was fiercely critical of the court for directing its first investigations at the Bosnian Serbs' political heads and military leaders and their sitting president Milošević. This criticism largely ignored the facts that emerged from investigations pointing to widespread Serbian massacres. Notwithstanding, the criticism of the prosecutors in The Hague was joined by international lawyers and human rights activists after the NATO airstrikes on Serbia in response to reported human rights violations in Kosovo in the spring of 1999. Accusations of war crimes were levelled against the NATO states, while the war also prompted a heated debate on the legality and legitimacy of humanitarian military interventions. The 1999 NATO intervention against Serbia is a good example of the absence of criminal sanctions, even where, as in this case, it was almost universally recognized that the war was illegal under international law. Criticism of the appeal to supposedly universal justifications for Western intervention was particularly strident throughout the Third World, since the world has already had "five centuries to assess the longer-run effects of the use of brutal force, and the claim that these effects are largely positive has come to seem empirically dubious to more and more people".[13] The few attempts to challenge the legality of the NATO campaign against Serbia and other wars in court have been limited to complaints on the basis of domestic administrative and constitutional provisions and have often centred on the question of parliamentary reservation. A practice of prosecutions for the international crime of the waging of an aggressive war has, for a variety of jurisdictional and political reasons, not emerged so far. A separate comprehensive analysis of this issue, and in particular of the debate on the concept of 'Responsibility to Protect' – the obligation to intervene where human rights violations are occurring on a massive scale – would be warranted, but lies outside the scope of this book.

The failure to open formal investigations against those responsible for NATO's breaches of international law fuelled criticism of the selectivity of the prosecutions and the West's political instrumentalization of the ex-Yugoslavia tribunal and added to misgivings toward international criminal justice around the globe.

In April 2008 Carla Del Ponte published some of her impressions from her time as chief prosecutor at the tribunal for the former Yugoslavia.[14] In her book, Del Ponte addresses the accusations of political selectivity levelled against her for her failure to launch proceedings in relation to war crimes committed by NATO and her inaction in respect of the crimes of the Kosovar paramilitary independence movement Ushtria Çlirimtare e Kosovës ('UÇK', Kosovo Liberation Army). Quite apart from the question of the legality of the intervention itself, NATO was criticized for breaching international humanitarian law by bombing civilian targets. Prosecution authorities in The Hague received detailed reports from Amnesty International, Human Rights Watch, the Serbian government and the Russian parliament on almost 90 incidents in Kosovo and

---

13   Immanuel Wallerstein, *European Universalism: The Rhetoric of Power*, The New Press, New York, 2006, p. 74.

14   Carla Del Ponte, *Madame Prosecutor: Confrontations with Humanity's Worst Criminals and the Culture of Impunity*, Other Press, New York, 2009.

Serbia where NATO air strikes killed an estimated 1,200 civilians and injured over 5,000 more. NATO was accused of putting the civilian population at risk by failing to adequately distinguish between military and civilian targets. These attacks, as well as NATO's use of cluster bombs and depleted uranium ammunition, were said to have been in violation of international humanitarian law. The bombings of a train in the Grdelica gorge on 12 April 1999, of a convoy of refugees on a street between Đjakovica and Dečani in western Kosovo on 14 April 1999, and on the Serbian television station RTS in Belgrade on 23 April 1999 came in for particularly harsh criticism.

In her book, Del Ponte agrees that some of these incidents, including the double bombing of a passenger train as it passed the railway bridge at the Grdelica gorge, would have merited legal action, but says that the unwillingness of NATO and its allies to co-operate led her to conclude that taking action on these crimes would exceed the tribunal's political resources. Not only would this attempt have ended in failure, she says, but it would also have made it impossible for the prosecution to continue to investigate and prosecute the crimes committed by local parties during the wars of the 1990s.[15] Del Ponte wrote this account eight years after she had made the decision not to open formal proceedings against perpetrators of possible NATO crimes in June 2000. At the time, she based her decision on the divided legal opinions of the expert team tasked with preliminarily examining the allegations against NATO. The team concluded that the legal basis of the accusations was not sufficiently certain and that it was unlikely that sufficient evidence could be found to secure convictions. Instead of recommending the opening of an investigation, the team somewhat dubiously relied on NATO press releases, claiming that these were generally trustworthy. When pressed by the team to give more information on specific incidents and allegations, NATO gave only very general answers. Criticism was rightly levelled at the team for finding that it was unnecessary to focus on individual incidents on the basis that NATO's precautionary measures aimed at avoiding civilian casualties worked in a very high percentage of cases. The fact, the team argued, that that precautionary measures had not worked in a small number of cases did not necessarily mean they were generally inadequate. The logic behind this finding seems to imply that there can be no action taken

---

[15] *Ibid.*, p. 60.

on war crimes where these were not part of a plan or a widespread commission of crimes.[16]

This approach, as documented in Del Ponte's memoirs, shows the hazards of the *ad hoc* courts' fundamental dependence on the UN, the major powers and NATO, which entails that the tribunals cannot achieve results without their support.[17]

Supporters of the ex-Yugoslavia tribunal argue in its defence that the prosecution of NATO war crimes would not have fit under the mandate of the court with its focus on the most severe crimes and the pursuit of those most responsible for such crimes. Even if this analysis is accepted, it remains the case that before discontinuing proceedings, the prosecution should have conducted a comprehensive investigation of the incidents in question and, as warranted, referred the cases to the appropriate national prosecution authorities.

Del Ponte describes the proceedings against sections of the UÇK as the most frustrating experience of her time at the tribunal. She recounts meeting the families of kidnapped and missing persons and the relatives' disappointment at the decision not to pursue investigations into the whereabouts of their loved ones. She also describes her investigations into the removal of the organs of Serbian prisoners and how witnesses called to give evidence for the prosecution became targets of bomb attacks and other acts of violence in Kosovo. Police officers involved in the investigation were murdered and a police building belonging to the UN Interim Administration Mission in Kosovo was attacked. After the memoirs were published, these detailed accounts prompted the Council of Europe to set up a parliamentary inquiry. The assembly's final report by the Swiss prosecutor, Dick Marty, detailed numerous suspected crimes by members of the UÇK and called for the resumption of investigations. In the report, Marty emphasizes that there cannot be one justice for the winners and another for the losers. In any conflict, all perpetrators must be brought to justice for the crimes they have committed, regardless of what side they

---

[16] A comprehensive critique of the findings of the ICTY Review Committee can be found, for example, in Paolo Benvenuti, "The ICTY Prosecutor and the Review of the NATO Bombing Campaign against the Federal Republic of Yugoslavia", in *European Journal of International Law*, 2001, vol. 12, no. 3, pp. 503–529.

[17] See also Bill Bowring, *The Degradation of the International Legal Order? The Rehabilitation of Law and the Possibility of Politics*, Routledge-Cavendish, Abingdon, 2008, pp. 52 ff.

---

were on and what political role they played. In the spring of 2014, the Kosovar parliament decided to extend the European Union Rule of Law Mission in Kosovo, leaving the way open for judicial investigations into the claims.

The ex-Yugoslavia tribunal's failure to investigate all incidents out of political deference to NATO and its allies left the court's reputation weakened. But that was not the only reason the court was disliked by many. While the court initially mainly pursued Serbian suspects, albeit without going after senior army commanders,[18] chief prosecutor Del Ponte pressed charges against members of the Croatian army for their roles in Operation Storm. Once again the person ultimately responsible for these crimes, the Croatian president Franjo Tuđman, managed to escape punishment entirely.

Of those convicted by the tribunal at the time of writing, 50 were Serbs and 13 were Croats, while the smaller parties to the conflict were relatively under-represented among the convicted, with just six Bosnians, two Albanians and two Macedonians facing punishment. According to current chief prosecutor Serge Brammertz, these imbalances are in part attributable to the unpredictability of the criminal proceedings. When there are only a small number of defendants from one of the conflict parties, these proceedings become laden with great symbolical significance; cases that end in acquittals may erroneously be seen by some observers as exoneration for the entire party to the conflict.[19]

One thing the court's diverse critics agree on is that the charges and proceedings against Milošević were defective in a number of aspects. Among other shortcomings, the court attempted to address three separate and highly complex sets of facts within one trial. It also proved fatal that Milošević was the sole defendant in the case; once he died, the proceedings were effectively rendered useless.[20]

---

[18] For a critique of this see Marko Attila Hoare, "Genocide in Bosnia and the Failure of International Justice", pp. 8 ff., see *supra* note 12, who discusses what he claims has been an imbalance in the amount of prosecution resources invested in pursuing Serbian perpetrators as compared to the percentage of war deaths attributable to the Serbs.

[19] Ronen Steinke, "Aus schwarz und weiß wird grau", in *Süddeutsche Zeitung*, 30–31 July 2011.

[20] Marko Attila Hoare, "Genocide in Bosnia and the Failure of International Justice", pp. 11 ff., see *supra* note 12.

5.2.   The UN Criminal Tribunal for Rwanda

The second *ad hoc* tribunal, the International Criminal Tribunal for Rwanda, was established on the basis of Security Council Resolution 995 in November 1994. Its headquarters are located in Arusha, Tanzania and its subject-matter jurisdiction extends to crimes against humanity, war crimes and genocide committed in Rwanda between 1 January and 31 December 1994. The work of the tribunal is coming to a close at the time of writing. A so-called residual mechanism has taken over the last pending appeals proceedings and the goal is to finalize case-work and any wrapping-up by the end of 2015. To date, 95 persons have faced charges. Of these, 14 have been acquitted and 55 convicted. Four accused remain at large, while the other cases have been referred to national jurisdictions or discontinued after the deaths of the defendants. The accused included Jean Paul Akayesu, the first person to be convicted of genocide by an international court since the Genocide Convention entered into force in 1951 in a decision that has been at the centre of the legal debate on the issue. The former prime minister of Rwanda, Jean Kambanda, was also convicted of genocide by the tribunal.

The legal situation remains unclear within Rwanda where, for over a decade, tens of thousands of suspects have been waiting, some under inhumane conditions, for their trials before domestic courts. While the primary responsibility for prosecuting the genocidaires rightly lies with Rwanda, this example also shows some of the problems with this approach. The state is struggling to cope with the volume of cases – as any state in that situation would – but also lacks the necessary infrastructure to complete the prosecutions, and has thus relied on *gacaca*, a traditional form of community justice, to help process the case load. The Tutsi regime headed by President Paul Kagame stands criticized for prosecuting only the crimes committed on the Hutu side and for attempting to instrumentalize the trials for political gain. Serious allegations have been made against the Rwandan army in connection with war crimes committed after the end of the genocide in Rwanda and in eastern Congo under the rule of Kagame. No indictments have yet occurred in relation to these crimes. This issue has been played out within Rwanda's criminal courts and has also cropped up as part of the criminal proceedings ongoing in Europe. Carla Del Ponte, originally installed as chief prosecutor for both tribunals, lost her mandate for the Rwanda tribunal after she suggested that her office should step up efforts to pursue suspects from within the current Tutsi government. She later accused supporters of the government, including the USA, of forcing her out of office to protect their political interests.

Parallel to these proceedings, almost one hundred criminal proceedings have been launched in European courts against individuals suspected of involvement in the 1994 Rwandan genocide. In 2001 a Belgian court sentenced four accused to between 12 and 20 years in prison. In February 2014 the Higher Regional Court in Frankfurt convicted a former Rwandan mayor to 14 years' imprisonment for aiding and abetting murder. In March 2014 the first of the French trials relating to the genocide came to an end with the sentencing of former Rwandan secret service head Pascal Simbikangwa to 25 years in prison.

As part of an investigation into a massacre of Hutus, the Spanish judiciary is investigating a number of members of the Rwandan government. These proceedings came in for criticism from Rwanda but also triggered harsh criticism from the African Union of the concept of universal jurisdiction in general. As a result, the European Union and the African Union agreed to jointly set up an expert commission. The commission's 2009 report failed, however, to make a significant contribution on the practice of universal jurisdiction.

5.3. Outcome of the Yugoslavia and Rwanda Tribunals

The two tribunals have a somewhat chequered record. There has been well-founded criticism for making political decisions to avoid prosecuting certain groups and senior figures. Yet both tribunals did enjoy certain successes. For the Croatian writer Slavenka Drakulić, the Balkan wars of the 1990s were made possible by the pervasive silence surrounding the Second World War, in combination with the official version of the events of 1939 to 1945.[21] She describes "how easy it is to start a war in the absence of facts"[22] when political leaders hijack the memories of people by obscuring them with popular mythology to stir up hatred. Her fear is that "if the truth is not established about the so-called 'war for the homeland', the next generation will one day find themselves in exactly the same situation as my post-Second World War generation".[23] For this reason she

---

[21] Slavenka Drakulić, *They Would Never Hurt a Fly: War Criminals on Trial in The Hague*, Penguin, London, 2004.

[22] *Ibid.*, p. 13.

[23] *Ibid.*, p. 14.

is in favour of carrying out extensive criminal proceedings into the conflict. That this should occur in The Hague is due to fact that the "former Yugoslav states were either unable or unwilling to prosecute their own war criminals".[24] Right-wing opponents of the tribunal in Croatia and Serbia saw it as a "political instrument established to punish and humiliate their country".[25] Until the truth about the war is established, she writes, the trials in The Hague and even those before local courts "will be seen as an injustice to the 'war heroes'. There is no justice without truth [...]".[26] As things stand, she wrote in 2003, "justice simply has to come from The Hague or it will not come at all".[27] Yet this still does not tell us more about the kind of impact that criminal trials in international courts have on the affected communities.

Both tribunals can be credited with making the best out of their challenging circumstances. They were set up on an *ad hoc* basis in an effort by the great powers, and particularly the veto powers, to score political points. At the time of their establishment, the UN Security Council did not foresee that they would grow into relatively functional courts or that they would continue with their work for over a decade. This lack of commitment of its founders was just one of the obstacles facing the courts. Every move they made was met with scepticism and often outright hostility by the rival conflict groups in the Balkans and Rwanda. Despite this, both courts were able to make at least some use of the leeway they had been granted and prove to the world that it is possible to organize a lasting international form of criminal jurisdiction. The courts laid important foundations for the subsequent development of the theory and practice of international criminal law, for instance, through their decisions on the elements of genocide, the applicability of international humanitarian law in non-international armed conflict, and criminal liability for sexualized violence. In its groundbreaking 1998 Akayesu decision, the tribunal for Rwanda held that rape could be seen as an instrument of genocide and that sexual violence included not just forcible bodily penetration but also other acts involving an element of coercion. This category encompassed acts such as rape, sexual slavery, and forced prostitution and pregnancy.

---

[24] *Ibid.*

[25] *Ibid.*, p. 15.

[26] *Ibid.*, p. 16.

[27] *Ibid.*, p. 17.

In a number of cases (including those concerning the Čelebići prison camp and the defendants Furundžija and Kunarac), the ex-Yugoslavia tribunal held that rape represented a form of torture. This marked an important step forward in the development of the legal view of rape, an act initially treated as a violation of the property rights of a man, later as an attack on a woman's honour, and now as the gravest form of violence – torture.[28]

5.4. The Hybrid Tribunals

Since the second half of the 1990s a series of tribunals has been established at the international level that can be classified as hybrid tribunals or 'internationalized' courts. With the support of the international community, they have been set up on the basis of agreements, usually between the UN and the court's host state, and with a mixed composition of national and international staff. They are based in the country in which the crimes were committed, in part to facilitate and reduce the cost of access to evidence and because it is generally more convenient for those involved in the trial (defendants, witnesses and lawyers as well as ancillary proceedings). It was also hoped that holding the tribunals in the states concerned would make it easier to communicate the court proceedings to the affected local communities and thus increase acceptance of the tribunals' work. In most cases, however, these aims have not been achieved.

During the period of transitional UN administration in East Timor, special chambers were created at the district court in the capital city of Dili. The court was given jurisdiction over the international crimes committed in the period between January and October 1999 as East Timor sought independence from long-standing Indonesian occupation. Between 7,000 and 20,000 people fell victim to the conflict. The court's mandate, however, did not cover the period of Indonesian occupation stretching back to 1975 during which Indonesian forces committed grave human rights violations and killed an estimated third of the population. A total of 391 people were charged by the tribunal, 290 of whom were not present in the country. From 2000 to 2005 the court oversaw 55 separate proceed-

---

[28] Kelly D. Askin, "Prosecuting Wartime Rape and Other Gender-Related Crimes under International Law: Extraordinary Advances, Enduring Obstacles", in *Berkeley Journal of International Law*, 2003, vol. 21, no. 2, pp. 288–349.

ings resulting in 84 convictions and three acquittals.[29] Herbert D. Bow-man, one of the international prosecutors, has criticized the selectivity and injustice of the tribunal. The big fish, namely the Indonesian commanders, managed to escape punishment, he says, while the court went after the smaller players, namely the members of the militia in East Timor.[30]

In 2002 Sierra Leone and the UN signed an agreement to establish a Special Tribunal in Freetown. The tribunal has tried 13 defendants for their roles in the most egregious war crimes and crimes against humanity committed during the country's civil war. No investigations were made into the similar grave crimes committed in neighbouring Liberia. The former Liberian president Charles Taylor, who was tried in Freetown for his involvement in the commission of war crimes in Sierra Leone, should by all accounts also have been held accountable for atrocities committed in his own country. For security reasons, Taylor's trial was moved to The Hague where he was convicted by the tribunal in May 2012 and sentenced to 50 years' imprisonment. This decision was affirmed by the appeals chamber in September 2013.

The genocide in Cambodia between 1975 and 1979, in which an estimated 1.5 million people lost their lives, is the subject of investigation by a further tribunal in Phnom Penh. The Extraordinary Chambers in the Courts of Cambodia, as the court is known, came into being only after lengthy negotiations between Cambodia and the UN and continues to be a source of controversy as the Cambodian government regularly intervenes in the court proceedings. Initially, only five surviving leaders of the Khmer Rouge ultimately faced charges. For political reasons no charges were brought against any currently powerful figures suspected of having committed crimes against humanity during the Khmer Rouge period.[31] Expert observers say that even today it would be possible to press charges against up to 10,000 participants in the Cambodian genocide. The first trial ended with the conviction of Kaing Guek Eav, also known as Duch, the former head of the Khmer Rouge torture prisons, who was sentenced to life imprisonment by the appeals chamber in February 2012. The second major trial of four senior Khmer Rouge commanders began in De-

---

[29] On the hybrid tribunals in general, see Anja Jetschke, "Der Kaiser hat ja gar keine Kleider an! – Strafverfolgung durch hybride Tribunale", in *Friedenswarte* 2011, vol. 86, nos. 1–2, pp. 101–131; on East Timor, p. 121.

[30] Quoted in *ibid.*, p. 124.

[31] *Ibid.*, p. 121.

---

cember 2011. Proceedings against one of the commanders were abandoned due to the death of the accused. A further case was abandoned after the defendant was held to be unfit for trial. The remaining two accused, Nuan Chea and Khieu Samphan, were both convicted of crimes against humanity in the context of the forcible transfer of the entire population of Phnom Penh to rural Cambodia in April 1975 and sentenced to life imprisonment in August 2014. Their convictions are being appealed by the defence at the time of writing, with proceedings in further trials of the same accused in respect of other atrocities pending. In March 2015 three more Khmer Rouge cadres were charged with homicide, crimes against humanity and war crimes in two other cases. The identity of two further suspects remains confidential.

Following an illegal war of aggression against Iraq, the Supreme Iraqi Criminal Tribunal was set up in December 2003 as part of the US occupation of the country. The court's subject-matter jurisdiction encompasses crimes against international law committed between the Ba'ath Party's takeover on 17 July 1968 and 1 May 2003, the date when an official end of hostilities was declared. The establishment of the tribunal was widely criticized in Iraq and elsewhere. The domestic judges on the bench had been trained by Britain and the USA, and were to carry out their duties on the basis of procedural and substantive provisions similar to those relied on by the ICC. The suspicion that these judges were acting at the behest or even as puppets of the occupying powers was reinforced by the fact that the court sat – for security reasons – within a restricted military zone in Baghdad with only limited access for the public and those involved in the proceedings. The trial of the former Iraqi dictator Saddam Hussein came in for particularly harsh criticism on account of the retroactive application of the court's statute, the retroactive introduction of the death penalty, the limited defence rights of the accused, and the haste with which the trial was conducted from the beginning right up to Hussein's execution on 30 December 2006. The occupying powers may have feared that a more thorough examination of Saddam Hussein's crimes would have revealed the political and military complicity of Western states.

In May 2007 a special tribunal was set up in respect of the murder of the Lebanese prime minister Rafic Hariri on 14 February 2005 and the possible involvement of foreign states, such as Syria. The tribunal was unique in that it was tasked not with investigating crimes against international law but with uncovering the truth about a single case of political murder. The trial began in January 2014 in Leidschendam, a suburb of The Hague, in the absence of the four defendants, who remain at large. In February 2014 the *in absentia* trial of a fifth defendant was joined with the main trial and the prosecutor gave its opening statement in June of that year. The distinguished Lebanese lawyer Mohamed Mattar takes a critical view of the proceedings, claiming that all UN actions in the region should be regarded as suspect since the West applies a double standard: an international tribunal was set up to investigate Hariri's murder, while no such efforts were made in relation to the 1,300 civilians killed during the 2006 Israeli military operations in southern Lebanon.[32] The work of the tribunal is also the subject of fierce political debate within Lebanon. The court has been denounced by Hezbollah, suspected of having been involved in Hariri's murder, as little more than a US plot to undermine their party.[33] The financing of the Special Tribunal by the Hariri family and by individuals close to the former French president Jacques Chirac has raised further doubts about the independence of the court.

These tribunals are born out of a catch-22 situation. On the one hand, national justice systems generally lack the political will and/or organizational capacity to prosecute such large-scale crimes in accordance with the rules of due process. Yet, in the eyes of the affected communities, internationalizing the courts risks reducing the legitimacy of the trials. According to the political scientist Anja Jetschke, the chances of a tribunal (as opposed to some other accountability mechanism) being set up is higher the more the power balance favours the former victims of state repression and the smaller the possibility that they themselves will face prosecution.[34] The jurisdiction of such tribunals tends to be limited in a way that is difficult to reconcile with principles of fairness as it extends only to crimes that occurred within a sometimes arbitrarily delimited time frame.[35] Political factors determine the choice of defendants who usually

---

[32] Reported in Alain Gesh, "Kein kurzer Prozess im Libanon", in *Le Monde Diplomatique*, February 2011, p. 17.

[33] *Ibid.*

[34] Jetschke, 2011, p. 103 f., see *supra* note 29.

[35] Jetschke demonstrates this by using the examples of Cambodia (*ibid.*, pp. 109 ff.), where the tribunal did not have jurisdiction over the crimes committed during the first civil war between 1966 and 1975 causing an estimated 500,000 to 600,000 deaths, nor over the war that led to the removal of the Khmer Rouge and killed between 225,000 and 1.16 million people, nor the phase between 1991 and 1999. In East Timor (p. 112 f.), the civil war in 1975 with around 100,000 victims in which the current government party, Frente

comprise formerly high-ranking individuals who no longer wield political influence. More numerous and significant trials can be expected in situations where there is a low risk of proceedings affecting the current political power structures in the country in question.[36] The evidence, she says, suggests that the rhetoric of an 'end to impunity' is not matched by reality. In her research, she instead encountered selective prosecutions that are divided along winner–loser lines while impunity continues to be rife.[37]

It appears that the political compromises reached between the international community (usually represented by the UN) and the affected states in the course of the establishment of the hybrid *ad hoc* tribunals has led to a high degree of horizontal and vertical selectivity of prosecutions. The ICC as a permanent, universal, international criminal court seems the best bet to rectify this situation. Whether this global court has lived up to expectations is examined below.

Revolucionária de Timor-Leste Independente, played a significant role and the crimes committed by the occupying Indonesians between 1975 and 1999 claiming an estimated 183,000 victims (around a third of the total population) were excluded from prosecutions. A similar phenomenon occurred in Sierra Leone (pp. 113 ff.), where the work of the tribunal was arbitrarily limited to a short period (2000–2005) of the civil war that had been ongoing since 1991.

[36] *Ibid.*, p. 122.

[37] *Ibid.*, p. 125.

6

From Videla to Rumsfeld:
Last Hope Universal Jurisdiction?

Since the ex-Yugoslavia tribunal was established in 1993, international criminal courts have dealt with just a tiny fraction of the many grave human rights violations committed throughout the 1970s, 1980s and 1990s. This is partly because the global powers were rarely able to reach a consensus on appropriate action, and without the agreement of the UN Security Council no prosecutions could be undertaken by international tribunals. There is, however, another avenue for the exercise of global criminal justice: criminal proceedings in national courts. National proceedings are effective at two levels. While their decisions have direct ramifications within the domestic legal sphere, they also contribute to the formation of customary international law and the creation of a global system of justice. In this way, they play an important supplementary role to the international institutions, whose limited capacity and narrow jurisdictional scope mean that support from the national courts is much needed.[1] The majority of the crimes should indeed be investigated at the national level, as prosecutions should ideally take place in the countries where the crimes were committed or where the majority of the perpetrators are based. In theory, it would be possible to take such cases anywhere in the world, as murder and rape are criminalized essentially everywhere and many states even have criminal provisions on crimes against international law, including torture and war crimes. Yet, while criminal courts can be found in all parts of the world, political circumstances often make prosecutions impossible.

In many regions, such political considerations result in impunity for grave human rights violations. This kind of impunity has a long history, as previously demonstrated by the example of the massacres committed by colonial powers. By the 1990s at the latest some improvements to the global human rights situation had occurred, thanks to the creation of vari-

---

[1]   See Hubert Thierry, "The European Tradition in International Law: Georges Scelle", in *European Journal of International Law*, 1990, vol. 1, no. 1, p. 194; and Antonio Cassese, "Remarks on Scelle's Theory of 'Role Splitting' (dédoublement fonctionnel) in International Law", in *European Journal of International Law*, 1990, vol. 1, no. 1, p. 214.

ous international conventions and treaties for the protection of human rights.

While the international criminal tribunals were set up largely thanks to the efforts of state actors, it was mainly non-state actors such as human rights organizations and associations of victims and relatives as well as lawyers who were instrumental in advancing national prosecutions for human rights violations. Initial efforts to secure domestic investigations and prosecutions were spearheaded mainly by local movements. The Mothers of the Plaza de Mayo in Argentina are a shining example of this kind of local action – and not only on account of their ultimate success. At first, none of the human rights organizations from Argentina, Chile, Peru or Guatemala managed to overcome the impunity for the crimes committed by their countries in the 1970s and 1980s without external support. The situation only began to improve once the local groups linked up with transnational efforts.

The idea is not new. The Algerian independence movement also worked to mobilize international solidarity, while the protest actions around the world were used to draw attention to the injustices of the Vietnam War. But it was not until the 1980s and 1990s that transnational activism was able to benefit from new opportunities. When effective local remedies were inaccessible, it was now possible to turn to other bodies in a process referred to as 'scale shifting' by social scientists.[2] Whenever possible, these alternative mechanisms were foreign courts, but UN institutions, courts of opinion and other global remedies proved useful, too. In time, successful actions were taken not only by prosecution authorities in third-party states, but also through recourse to compensation cases – particularly in the USA – and the submission of complaints against offending states with the European and Inter-American Courts of Human Rights.

This practice, widely used today by non-governmental organizations ('NGO'), originated in the early 1980s with a series of historic civil cases on human rights violations before US courts. The innovative approach was not part of a strategic master plan, but a result of a chance discovery made while Rhonda Copelon and Peter Weiss from the New York-based Center for Constitutional Rights were considering how best to seek justice on behalf of the family of the Paraguayan torture victim Joelito

---

[2] Sidney Tarrow, *The New Transnational Activism*, Cambridge University Press, Cambridge, 2006.

Filartiga. The lawyers had learned that Filartiga's torturer was in the USA and came across the Alien Tort Claims Act, an 18th-century statute which had fallen into disuse, but which provided for the jurisdiction of US civil courts for extraterritorial violations of international law. The statute was originally designed to facilitate tort claims against pirates. Traditionally, these outlaws and not the perpetrators of state oppression had been seen as 'enemies of mankind' to be held to account transnationally. The courts were nonetheless open to a novel application of the law, so that human rights organizations were able to secure compensation for human rights violations committed outside of the USA in Filartiga's and many subsequent cases. This successful use of the Alien Torts Claims Act established the practice of universal jurisdiction in civil cases. The problem with the approach was that the success of each case hinged on finding a sympathetic court. The more powerful the respondent in the claim, the more the case had to contend with obstacles and intervention from the US and other governments as well as from the respondents which increasingly included big and resourceful companies. The objections raised against this practice are also applicable to the current debate on universal jurisdiction for criminal cases. Those who oppose such proceedings are critical of the unilateral nature of a state's decision to assume jurisdiction – in the absence of international consensus or regulation – over extraterritorial crimes in a way that interferes with the sovereignty of other states. A further objection is that the varying approaches of national courts to the application of international law would lead to its further fragmentation.

Among the most famous examples of transnational criminal prosecution for human rights violations are the trials of Adolf Eichmann and Ivan Demjanjuk in Jerusalem initiated by Israel, the work done by non-state actors such as the French lawyer Serge Klarsfeld, who represented French victims of Nazi persecution before German courts, and the efforts of solidarity groups from France and Italy who in the 1980s fought to initiate proceedings against members of the Argentine military in respect of the murder of Italian and French nationals.

6.1. European Cases against Pinochet, Videla and Rumsfeld

Cases taken to Spanish courts in the mid-1990s that concerned crimes committed during the military dictatorships in Argentina and Chile marked a significant development as to the transnational prosecution of international crimes.[3] The cases, which have come to be regarded as an unprecedented success of the Spanish investigative judge Baltasar Garzón and the human rights movement itself, started on 28 March 1996 with a criminal complaint issued by the Spanish prosecutor Carlos Castresana from the Spanish Union of Progressive Prosecutors. It concerned 38 predominantly Spanish victims of the Argentine dictatorship. Complaints were levelled against the generals Jorge Rafael Videla, Emilio Eduardo Massera and Antonio Domingo Bussi. Castresana was soon joined in his efforts by other progressive lawyers and activists from the Argentine expatriate community. This new network began systematically collecting information, looking for witnesses and victims, building cases and bringing them before the courts in Spain. On the basis of these investigations and the testimony of over two hundred witnesses, Garzón issued numerous arrest warrants for Argentine military officers. At the time, the political climate in Spain was conducive to such cases. Although the Spanish prosecution was initially inclined to accept the Argentine military's auto-amnesties and their justification that only isolated incidents of excessive violence had occurred, in a state of emergency necessary to defend the fatherland, this line of defence was strongly disputed by progressive sections of the Spanish public (who were reminded of the arguments put forward by Spanish right-wingers in defence of Francoist crimes).

Up to this point, almost everyone involved had envisaged that a successful outcome of such trials would occur in the forum states where the trials were taking place. The focus was firmly on domestic criminal prosecutions in countries such as Spain or France. Soon, however, problems arose due to the fact that in countries such as Germany, Belgium and Britain, where the exercise of universal jurisdiction is in principle a legal possibility, it is generally not permitted to conduct criminal proceedings and, in particular, to hand down convictions in the absence of the defendant. In such a constellation, the prosecution of international crimes is only an option if one or some of the defendants are present in the forum state or at least in a country where it is possible to have them arrested. The alternative would be to lodge an official extradition request with the home state, a procedure that has little chance of success given political considerations and the fact that many countries refuse to extradite their

---

[3]   See Wolfgang Kaleck, *Kampf gegen die Straflosigkeit: Argentiniens Militärs vor Gericht*, Verlag Klaus Wagenbach, Berlin, 2010.

own nationals. France and Italy do allow for trials and even convictions *in absentia*, but such proceedings raise concerns in relation to the rule of law since the defendant can only be guaranteed an effective defence if he or she is present in the courtroom. Such trials can, however, be of considerable importance to victims and the concerned public.

The problem for prosecution authorities in European states – who are often called on by human rights organizations to take up criminal proceedings on the basis of universal jurisdiction – is that while they might launch what are often highly complex investigations, they do not know if it will be possible to bring them to a satisfactory conclusion down the line. The objection that these cases are overly resource intensive is often raised by state prosecutors who are reluctant to take up difficult investigations, and by other commentators who for various reasons are sceptical of such proceedings. While at first glance this argument might seem to hold water, closer examination proves it to be unsound. The work of international tribunals including the ICC has already shown that comprehensive preliminary investigations are indispensable; without them it is impossible to secure arrest warrants, the arrest and detention of suspects or the opening of an official investigation. As such, anyone who wishes to see prosecutions occur in a given situation must be willing to launch preliminary investigations in acceptance of the risk that it might not be possible to bring the defendants before the courts in order to successfully conclude the case.

The success of the Spanish and European cases on Argentina and Chile, something that was far from guaranteed when Judge Garzón took up his investigations in 1996, can be traced back to a number of factors. In 2005 a Madrid court sentenced the Argentine naval officer Adolfo Scilingo to 640 years in prison for crimes against humanity, a sentence that was increased in 2007 to 1,084 years. Scilingo was the first of the officers involved in the crimes to give detailed testimony on the conditions within the notorious torture camp Escuela de la Mecánica de la Armada in Buenos Aires and the practice of death flights. Over the following years, the results of the Spanish investigations led to more arrests of Argentine officers in Italy, Mexico and Spain. After a series of further legal victories, the former Chilean dictator Augusto Pinochet was arrested in London on 16 October 1998 in response to a request by Judge Garzón. The case came before the British House of Lords who held in a landmark decision that in cases concerning torture, former heads of state were not entitled to enjoy immunity from prosecution in another state. It appeared that nothing could now stand in the way of Pinochet's extradition and trial in Spain. A fatal blow was dealt to this plan, however, on 2 March 2000, when the British government decided to allow Pinochet to travel home to Chile on health grounds.

The efforts of European prosecutors and courts to secure arrest warrants and extradition requests greatly increased the willingness of South American governments and prosecutors to deal with these crimes domestically. This phenomenon is now known as the Pinochet or Videla effect, a process in which lawyers and human rights organizations make creative use of transnational and national forums in order to circumvent domestic cultures of impunity. Since the end of the 1990s Chile has initiated and completed numerous criminal cases, while civil claims and asset seizure proceedings are currently ongoing against the Pinochet family. In Argentina, the amnesty and immunity laws that had been in place for almost 20 years were finally lifted between 2003 and 2005. Since 2006 investigations have been launched into around 2,600 former members of the military and others involved in the crimes of the dictatorship, with around 550 convictions secured to date. While it is difficult to assess the extent to which these developments are due to the described judicial and political moves made with regard to investigations in Europe, the impact of transnational activities continues to be regarded, particularly in Argentina, as extremely useful and is still encouraged.

Motivated by these successes, networks of lawyers and human rights activists began to emerge towards the end of the 1990s and at the beginning of the 2000s with the aim of exchanging and co-operating on cases of transnational criminal prosecution for human rights violations. International groups such as Amnesty International, Human Rights Watch and the International Federation for Human Rights were joined by a range of regional groups working on issues in their own countries and regions. Efforts were made in Europe and elsewhere to secure the prosecution of suspects from over 50 countries. The Argentine professor of law Máximo Langer has listed over 1,051 criminal complaints filed under the banner of universal jurisdiction in Belgium, France, Spain, Britain, Germany and elsewhere up to 2009.[4] A substantial percentage of these, however, were

---

[4] Máximo Langer, "The Diplomacy of Universal Jurisdiction: The Political Branches and the Transnational Prosecution of International Crimes", in *American Journal of International Law*, 2011, vol. 105, no. 1, pp. 1–49.

submitted with minimal preparatory work, some of them in cases where there was no prospect of a legal success or without adequate factual evidence, meaning that it would not be particularly helpful to draw any substantial conclusions from these statistics.

6.2. The Case of the Former Chadian Dictator Hissène Habré

For over a decade, human rights organizations from Chad worked with Human Rights Watch to pursue legal action against the former dictator of Chad, Hissène Habré, who is known as 'Africa's Pinochet'. They sought to hold Habré accountable for his role in the torture and murder of 40,000 oppositionists. In 1990 Habré fled from Chad to Senegal. Following Senegal's initial refusal to prosecute Habré, victims lodged criminal complaints against him in 2000 in Belgium, which at the time offered the most promising legal framework for victims of human rights violations. An international arrest warrant was issued in 2005, prompting a turn of events that would make Habré's case one of the most significant on a global scale.

Within Africa, criticism had been steadily building in relation to the actions of Belgium and other European countries in respect of the prosecution of international crimes committed in Africa. The government of the DR Congo, which was embroiled in a similar case involving former Congolese foreign minister Abdoulaye Yerodia Ndombasi, lodged an ultimately successful complaint with the International Court of Justice in The Hague. The Court found that Belgium's issuance of an arrest warrant against a serving foreign minister represented an unlawful impingement upon Congolese sovereignty since it interfered with that minister's capacity to exercise his duties. Yerodia was therefore held to be immune from Belgian prosecution.

Although the case of Habré was different in respect of a possible immunity from prosecution, as he was no longer in office and survivors' NGOs were able to convince the Chadian government to formally waive any claims of immunity, the African Union and Senegal kept dragging their feet. The African Union finally decided to have the former dictator put on trial in Africa instead of Europe. Senegal then made the necessary legislative changes and entered into lengthy negotiations with the international community to secure the millions of dollars required to conduct the proceedings. Yet despite all requirements being met and the necessary permissions being granted, the trial of Habré never occurred, a failure for which only rather spurious reasons were provided. Following significant international pressure and a change in government in Senegal, a Special Tribunal was eventually established to deal with the alleged crimes of Habré. In July 2013 he was charged with crimes against humanity and placed under provisional arrest. Some 1,015 of his victims have registered as civil parties. The investigative phase, during which the investigative judges have heard about 2,500 witnesses and victims and analysed ample evidence, was closed with a decision to confirm the charges in February 2015. The trial phase is scheduled to start in the summer of 2015.

The Habré case is particularly significant as it represents a success-ful effort by human rights activists to extend the practice of universal ju-risdiction to other continents. An African case of mass violence will now be brought to trial in Africa. This frees the case from any semblance of neocolonialism and lends the proceedings more legitimacy. This case also bolsters the concept of pursuing criminal prosecutions for such crimes in third states as it marks the spread of the practice to another region of the world outside of Europe. Senegal's readiness to carry out the proceedings – in accordance with the resolutions of the African Union – could be an important step towards the global application of universal jurisdiction for severe human rights violations. Furthermore, after the Special Tribunal's prosecutor had in vain requested the indictment of five former cadres of Habré's administration, two of these have been convicted on charges of murder and torture in Chad alongside another 18 former officials on 25 March 2015. The Chadian judges also ordered the compensation of the 7,000 victims who participated in the proceedings and the construction of a monument to those murdered under Habré's rule. This impressively demonstrates the potential of transnational prosecutions to trigger the end-ing of a long-standing culture of impunity in societies that have suffered from mass violence in the past – the Pinochet Videla effect has reached Africa.

Human rights organizations have been less successful in their at-tempts to bring about prosecutions for crimes committed by the veto pow-ers which have not ratified the Statute of the ICC. Russia, however, has subjected itself to the jurisdiction of the European Court of Human Rights and is regularly held to account in Strasbourg for human rights violations committed in Chechnya. Also, in connection with the torture of a Chechen oppositionist, a criminal complaint was lodged in Austria in the summer of 2008 against the Chechen president Ramzan Kadyrov. Kadyrov had been planning to travel to Austria to see the Russian football team play in the European Championship. Given the amount of evidence against him, the Austrian judiciary would have been obliged to act once Kadyrov entered the country, but instead blocked every attempt to pursue the proceedings. The case later collapsed when the torture survivor who was the instigator of the criminal complaint, and the key witness in the case, was assassinated in broad daylight on a street in Vienna in January 2009. He had previously filed a complaint against Russia before the European Court of Human Rights.

6.3. Investigations into US Military and Police Officials

After criminal complaints were lodged with Belgian authorities in the spring 2003 against General Tommy Franks, the US commander overseeing the invasion of Iraq, Belgium introduced changes to its universal jurisdiction law which make proceedings more difficult for victims of human rights violations. The USA had exerted huge pressure on Belgium, threatening to move NATO headquarters from Brussels and stating that Belgium's status as an international centre was at risk if Belgium failed to restrict the scope of these laws. Following these threats, the proceedings against Franks were swiftly discontinued and, within a few months, Belgium had restricted the laws to such an extent that prosecutions could essentially only be pursued for crimes against international law in cases affecting Belgian nationals.

The experience with Belgium has since acted as a cautionary tale for some within the human rights movements. In 2004 the first major criminal complaints were lodged in Germany against the former US Secretary of Defense Donald Rumsfeld and other senior political and military figures in connection with torture at the Abu Ghraib detention centre in Iraq. Amnesty International criticized the approach of those involved in making the complaints, arguing that they were endangering the fledgling practice of universal jurisdiction in Europe, a practice that should initially be tested out only on less prominent defendants. In its view, it was important to avoid the kind of political confrontations that might lead to setbacks that could cause states to limit the scope of their laws as Belgium had. The instigators of the criminal complaints, who included this author, countered that if the concept of universal jurisdiction did not enable perpetrators of human rights violations from powerful states such as the USA to be brought to justice, it was not a legal practice worth defending. The most useful approach, we argued, is to work to ensure that the law is applied universally and equally in every case.

The criminal complaints filed in Germany in 2004 and 2006 and similar cases in France in 2007, Spain in 2009 and Switzerland in February 2011 were all directed against the senior politicians, lawyers and military officers involved in implementing the US torture programme after 11 September 2001. They mainly centred on the torture conflict-related detainees in Iraq and of terror suspects in Guantánamo. When photographs emerged in the spring of 2004 showing the abuse of detainees at Abu Ghraib, a number of inquiries were carried out in the USA by the government, Congress and the military. The inquiries resulted in the publication of a range of internal documents on the issue of abuse, and it soon became evident that the incidents in Abu Ghraib were only the tip of the iceberg.

It emerged that the torture methods that had come to light had been used in nearly all of the detention centres where the USA and its allies held terror suspects and prisoners of war. Memoranda that were released showed that by the winter of 2001–2002, the US government and heads of the intelligence services had drafted legal justifications denying detainees their basic rights under the Geneva Conventions and depriving them of the protection against torture. Attempts had also been made to redefine the term of torture in order to legitimize methods such as waterboarding and stress positions, practices that had long been considered to constitute torture when used by the Soviet Union during the Cold War. Despite numerous documented cases of torture, some of which even resulted in the death of the detainees (Human Rights Watch alone has documented 350 cases of abuse), investigations have been launched in only a small number of cases. The most senior individual to be prosecuted was Lieutenant Colonel Steve Jordan. The Bush administration had claimed that the Abu Ghraib scandal was an isolated event, the work of a few 'bad apples' who did not share American values. The public debate centred on the army unit responsible for the night shift at Abu Ghraib; Private Lynndie England and Specialist Charles Graner soon became the faces of US torture. Human rights organizations such as Human Rights Watch (through, for example, the 2011 report "Getting Away with Torture", the Center for Constitutional Rights ('CCR') and the ECCHR from Berlin, continue to seek criminal prosecutions against the more senior figures in the affair.

Not long after taking office, President Barack Obama made the decision not to pursue criminal proceedings against his predecessor or against former Vice President Cheney or Rumsfeld. As such, the only remaining option is to pursue investigations in third-party states, for example in Europe.

6.4. European Efforts to Date: A Mixed Record

Criminal proceedings within European states have had varying levels of success. Most criminal complaints lodged with European authorities were dismissed on what were often legally spurious bases. It soon became clear that the US government and its diplomats were engaged in concerted efforts to influence the course of justice in the courts of its European allies. This was certainly true for cases concerning the CIA extraordinary rendition programme underway in Italy, Germany and Spain and for cases relating to secret US detention centres in Poland, Lithuania and Romania.

In the case of the abduction and torture of the Egyptian citizen Abu Omar in 2004, it became public knowledge in 2010 that the US government had been interfering with their Italian counterparts to prevent the conviction of involved CIA officials. Notwithstanding, 22 CIA officials and the US Air Force Colonel Joseph L. Romano III were convicted and sentenced *in absentia* at first instance in 2009. These convictions were affirmed by the Appeals Court of Milan in 2010. Five Italian suspects had their cases dismissed by the court of first instance due to concerns about state secrets. In 2012 the Court of Cassation ordered to reopen these proceedings, only to have its decision overturned by the Italian Constitutional Court in 2014. The convictions of the five accused which had in the meantime been issued by the Appeals Court of Milan were therefore quashed. In April 2013 Romano was pardoned by the Italian president Giorgio Napolitano who cited Obama's termination of the rendition programme, concerns about Italy's relations with the USA, and a new Italian law that allows renunciation of criminal jurisdiction over crimes committed by NATO personnel deployed abroad as reasons for his pardon.

In Germany, prosecution authorities in Munich have launched investigations into the kidnapping of the German national Khaled El Masri and a Munich court has issued international arrest warrants for a dozen CIA agents implicated in the case. Just like in Italy, the German government has refrained from requesting the USA to extradite the suspects. In

2010 documents released through WikiLeaks indicate that discussions were held between US diplomats and representatives of the German and Spanish judiciaries. Despite the plentiful evidence indicating that extraordinary rendition was overseen at the very highest levels, no action has been taken against those responsible for the programme at the most senior level, such as the former CIA director George Tenet. Notwithstanding, after the 2014 publication of the summary of report by the US Senate Intelligence Committee on torture by the CIA and another criminal complaint submitted by the CCR and the ECCHR, the German Office of the Federal Prosecutor has opened a monitoring procedure under which it is gathering evidence and that could eventually result in a fully-fledged criminal investigation.

Another recent success story concerns a French investigation into crimes committed in Guantánamo which was initiated in reaction to a criminal complaint submitted by French citizens and former Guantánamo inmates Nizar Sassi and Mourad Benchellali. At first, the investigation had been characterized by the procrastination and lack of determination which are typical for this kind of high-profile case involving foreign officials as suspects. Various requests for assistance to the US had remained unanswered and the investigating judges rejected the civil parties' request to summon the former Guantánamo commander Geoffrey Miller. In March 2015, however, the Court of Appeals granted the civil parties' appeal against this decision and ordered the summoning of Miller.

There have been a number of triumphs. The proceedings have ensured that the actions of the USA and its allies have been extensively and publicly discussed across Europe. Some US suspects have cancelled their European travel plans to avoid the risk of arrest. In 2004–2005, Rumsfeld let it be known that he would not be travelling to Germany until the proceedings against him had been fully concluded. In February 2011 former president Bush cancelled a private trip to Switzerland after criminal complaints were lodged against him there. CIA agents involved in the rendition of terror suspects have been explicitly warned against travelling to Europe for fear of arrest. In July 2013 the CIA official Robert Seldon Lady, who had been convicted in connection with the kidnapping of Abu Omar in Italy, was initially detained in Panama at Italian request. He was, however, released the next day and flew to the USA, as there was no extradition agreement between Italy and Panama.

Even a cursory examination reveals a substantial difference in the response to US actions after 11 September 2001, on the one hand, and the accusations made in connection with the Vietnam War, the US secret service involvement in Operation Condor carried out by South American dictatorships, or the US interventions in Central America, on the other. The most significant change is that legal scholars and the wider public are now measuring US actions against the applicable national and international laws. Those at the Pentagon and the White House who are responsible for US crimes became increasingly worried by the risk of criminal prosecutions. This is evidenced by a number of factors: the numerous attempts made to destroy or conceal the evidence of their activities, the recourse to blatantly erroneous legal memoranda by White House lawyers purporting to justify illegal interrogation methods and the establishment of extensive immunity from prosecution through the passage of the Military Commission Act of 2006. Another new feature is the willingness of international and foreign justice systems to undertake genuine investigations into these crimes to the extent that suspects have to reckon with the possibility of arrest should they ever set foot on the continent.

Similar controversies and interventions by diplomats and governments arose in the context of cases against Israeli politicians and military officers accused of crimes against the Palestinians.

But the US and Israeli governments were not the only states to oppose the proceedings in Spain; China and the African Union both added their voices to the criticisms of the Spanish judiciary's approach to universal justice. Despite these controversies, the many proceedings initiated in Spain received very little publicity, both in Spain and further afield, and this even holds true for the more successful cases such as those on the genocide of indigenous populations in Guatemala and the murder of Salvadorian oppositionists in the 1980s. Even the groundbreaking achievements of the Spanish judiciary as to crimes of the dictatorships in Argentina and Chile failed to garner the interest they might have warranted. Only when accusations were levelled against investigative judge Garzón himself for an alleged perversion of justice and other offences did most of the Spanish public begin to pay attention.

Garzón had made a number of powerful enemies among politicians in the socialist and conservative parties in Spain from his time spent investigating domestic corruption and state crime. The charges against Garzón – which led to his suspension from the bench in the spring of

2010 – emerged after he initiated investigations into the crimes of the Franco dictatorship and sought to examine the fate of almost 150,000 people who disappeared during that period. Suddenly, the kind of back-lash long feared by sceptics was happening in the very country that had been leading the way in international criminal justice. The fledgling human rights-based practice of transnational criminal law was now being curtailed by legislative reforms and the spurious removal from office of its main protagonist. This development was a particularly bitter blow to the movement.

The fact that Spain would resort to such authoritarian measures to quash investigations into its own dictatorial past only lent credibility to complaints from states involved in proceedings before Spanish courts that such cases were part of a neocolonialist scheme and represented a violation of their sovereignty. It seems as if criminals guilty of human rights violations no longer have to fear prosecution before Spanish courts. In February 2014 the parliament in Spain, a country that had once been a pioneer of the movement, passed a controversial reform placing strict limitations on the application of universal jurisdiction in Spanish courts. The law sets down comprehensive and complex requirements for the establishment of the jurisdiction of Spanish courts in cases of genocide, crimes against humanity and war crimes, and applies not only to all future cases but also to investigations that are currently ongoing. However, some hope persists in respect of a pending investigation into torture at Guantánamo. Against all odds, the investigating judge decided to keep the investigation active, a decision that was confirmed in an interlocutory appeal. Despite this Pyrrhic victory, the proceedings are still threatened to be discontinued on the basis of the new universal jurisdiction law once they reach the trial stage.

After a little over 15 years of criminal proceedings of international crimes in Europe, the interim results are mixed. At first glance, the findings are disheartening; of the 1,051 proceedings undertaken in Western Europe, only 32 proceeded to trial. And while the criminal complaints lodged in Europe were directed against a broad range of suspects from all over the world including China (44), Russia (3) and the USA (55), the trials that ultimately took place involved only suspects from Afghanistan, Argentina, DR Congo, the former Yugoslavia, Mauritania, Rwanda and

Tunisia as well as a small number of Nazi criminals.[5] The auspicious beginnings of the European prosecutions seen in the Argentina and Chile cases remain a lamentably isolated phenomenon. It is true, however, that a large number of cases on human rights violations are still underway, in particular in Argentina, cases that helped trigger a wave of legal action on state crimes throughout Latin America. These developments inspired human rights organizations in the West and in the Global South to pursue further cases. Nevertheless, European states still have a long way to go to develop a universal practice of international justice that would support and complement the efforts of the ICC.

The reasons for these shortcomings vary. The difficulties begin with the gathering abroad of evidence on what are generally state instruments of repression, evidence that must then be reproduced in criminal proceedings in compliance with European legal standards. The cases often involve the investigation of conflicts and dictatorships that have lasted for decades, which presents a significant practical and organizational burden. Further problems are presented by gaps in domestic legislation which often lacks laws specifically dealing with international crimes such as genocide, crimes against humanity and war crimes. In almost all countries there is a paucity of specialized criminal prosecutors and investigators, and prosecution authorities are often limited by the inadequate resources at their disposal. Witnesses from affected countries are often living in constant fear of attack from the groups responsible for the crimes in question and authorities abroad cannot guarantee their safety. Significant legal problems arise from the dilemma of hearing cases *in absentia*. In most cases, proceedings can be pursued only when the suspect is present in the state, yet when a suspect travels to Europe the prosecution authorities are generally unable to react quickly, as the preliminary evidence is not yet sufficient to warrant arrest or searches. Furthermore, suspects who hold high political office are shielded from prosecution by their immunity or through international agreements on the protection of diplomatic relations.

The greatest obstacle to prosecution, however, is a lack of political will. Prosecutions are only successful in cases everyone can agree on. These are either cases involving low-ranking suspects or defendants from weak and powerless states. A case that risks putting a state's political, economic or military interests at risk tends to end in one of two ways: ei-

---

[5]   *Ibid.*, p. 8.

ther the case will not be taken up by the judiciary in the first place, or sufficient political pressure will be exerted to suppress the proceedings. This is particularly true in countries where the justice system provides victims of human rights violations and human rights organizations with a strong say in criminal proceedings, and where investigative judges and prosecution authorities enjoy a significant degree of freedom to pursue cases as they see fit. As well as intervening politically in many cases, Belgium, Spain, France, Britain and others have all altered their laws to make it more difficult to prosecute perpetrators of crimes against international law against the will of the executive. In this way, states have restricted the scope of the relatively independent investigate judges and limited the rights of victims to join such proceedings. Just over 15 years after the very promising advances made in Spain, the development is reversing It is now increasingly difficult for human rights organizations to bring criminal cases in European courts against individuals responsible for torture and massacres around the world. Yet the practice of universal justice, whereby victims of human rights violations can have recourse to justice in their own countries or elsewhere, has taken a firm hold. Temporary setbacks such as those detailed above will not be enough to deter the people and groups involved in its progress.

7

_____

Could Do Better: The Practice of
International Criminal Law in Germany

Until the 1990s, the debate on international criminal law in Germany
mainly circled around the country's own criminal past – from German
culpability for colonial crimes committed against the Herero people in the
early 20th century in former German South West Africa, to the egregious
war crimes of the First World War and, finally, the Nazi extermination
policies. That Germany would not put on trial its nationals accused of international crimes was evidenced by the trials it carried out after the First
World War as part of the conditions set down by the Treaty of Versailles.
At the Leipzig trials, held between 1921 and 1927, not even the semblance of any serious attempt to mete out justice was created. The attempt
was stifled by the lack of political will in Germany to prosecute its war
criminals and the absence of sufficient pressure from the allies to hold
genuine trials.[1]

The application of international criminal law to these cases – had it
occurred – would have resulted in the convictions of many more German
perpetrators and potentially further reparations. The scepticism and open
hostility towards international criminal law harboured by the West German populace, its government and lawyers were to endure for a remarka-
bly long time, even after the immensely more egregious atrocities committed by Germany during the Second World War. For decades, West
Germany refused to sign up to the exception to the inadmissibility of ret-

_____

[1]   Germany refused to extradite almost 900 suspects wanted by the Allied forces. Instead it
was agreed that German war criminals should be tried before the *Reichsgericht* in Leipzig.
Only nine trials were carried out with a total of just 12 defendants. Six of these were acquitted while others came away with short prison sentences. The German government successfully resisted subsequent attempts to extradite German suspects. Gerd Hankel explains
that the failure to prosecute the massive German war crimes was down to a desire within
German political circles to right the perceived wrongs of the Peace Treaty of Versailles,
for which the "necessary pressure" was expected to be provided by the military that should
therefore not be alienated through prosecutions. Members of the German judiciary, who
had long sought recognition and acceptance by the country's elite, did not want to stand
apart. Gerd Hankel, *Die Leipziger Prozesse: Deutsche Kriegsverbrechen und ihre stra-
frechtliche Verfolgung nach dem Ersten Weltkrieg*, Hamburger Edition, Hamburg, 2003.

roactive criminal laws under Article 7 of the European Convention on Human Rights in respect of crimes against humanity. Unlike the German Democratic Republic ('GDR'), West Germany also refused to sign the Convention on the Non-Applicability of Statutory Limitations to War Crimes and Crimes Against Humanity.

This scepticism has now fallen away, a fact that is of little use in terms of prosecuting Nazi criminals since few are still alive. The trial and conviction of Ivan Demjanjuk, a former guard at the Sobibór concentration camp, attracted global attention in 2011. This case and similar prosecutions, like the criminal trial of a 93-year-old former SS member who was in charge of administrating the confiscated property of those murdered at Auschwitz initiated in April 2015, illustrate the current political desire to persist with prosecutions for such crimes. But the record of these trials is somewhat undermined by the fact that they generally concern only the surviving rank and file of the machinery of extermination, while scores of more senior perpetrators from the upper Nazi echelons managed to escape prosecution after the end of the war in 1945.

This issue applies not only to criminal proceedings. The rejection of legal arguments that favour the victims of international crimes is of continued relevance in a series of civil cases taken against the German state by victims of Nazi war crimes in Greece and Poland and former forced labourers and prisoners of war from Italy. Germany took a very restrictive position, arguing that the state immunity traditionally guaranteed under international law bars the bringing of individual civil compensation claims in foreign courts, even in cases of grave human rights violations. This position was ultimately affirmed by the International Court of Justice in 2012 in proceedings between Germany and Italy concerning the legality of compensation claims of victims of German war crimes that had been granted by Italian courts. The court did, however, not address whether the compensation claims of the victims were well founded in substance. Not surprisingly, Germany is until now unwilling to pay reparations to individual Greek and Italian war crimes survivors. In September 2013 the German Constitutional Court – despite finding constitutional issues regarding errors made during the respective foregoing civil proceedings – held that the civilian victims of the NATO bombing of the Serbian village of Varvarin were not entitled to compensation from Germany, as principal reason that a causal German involvement in the bombing could not be proven.

Although not concerning charges of international crimes in the traditional sense, it is certainly the case that the trials undertaken in connection with the crimes of the GDR to date have touched on a number of issues related to international criminal law. This is particularly so in respect of the trials as to liability of GDR lawyers and members of the *Politbüro*. The *Politbüro* case concerned the role of the GDR's political and military leadership in the killing of East German citizens at the border. That the court chose to convict the officials as indirect perpetrators on the basis of their domination over an organizational apparatus (*"mittelbare Täterschaft kraft Organisationsherrschaft"*) is another indication that these kinds of decisions are not always based solely on 'objective' legal arguments. Rather, courts often take the political decision if certain groups will be targeted for prosecution or not by drawing on legal doctrine. In this case, the doctrine of *"mittelbare Täterschaft kraft Organisationsherrschaft"* which had been developed in the context of Nazi crimes by the criminal lawyer Claus Roxin, and had not been relied on in decades, was resurrected in order to facilitate the convictions of senior GDR officials.

Since the 1990s the German criminal justice system has left behind its formerly purely domestic focus in respect of international criminal law and has worked particularly intensively on two extraterritorial cases: the genocide in Bosnia-Herzegovina and the crimes of the dictatorship in Argentina. German investigators co-operated closely with the ex-Yugoslavia tribunal; a total of 500 requests for assistance were issued in connection with the cases. Towards the end of the 1990s, German prosecutors opened around a hundred investigatory proceedings in connection with international crimes committed in the former Yugoslavia. The most significant case was one against Bosnian Serb Nikola Jorgić who was accused of killing 29 Muslim villagers and the unlawful detention and torture of Muslims. Jorgić was convicted of genocide by the Higher Regional Court in Düsseldorf in a decision that was subsequently affirmed by the German Federal Court of Justice and the Federal Constitutional Court and finally by the European Court of Human Rights in 2007. While the Bosnian-Serb cases were taken up mainly at the prosecution authorities' own initiative, in 1998 human rights organizations began to lodge criminal complaints for the first time in order to bring about prosecutions for crimes against international law.

Between 1998 and 2003 the specially formed human rights network Koalition gegen Straflosigkeit (Coalition against Impunity) submitted criminal complaints directed at almost 90 Argentine military and police officers on behalf of nearly 40 German and German-descendant victims of the Argentine military dictatorship. While the competent German prosecution authorities in Nuremberg-Fürth acted slowly at first, the investigations picked up momentum after two to three years when German prosecutors heard the testimonies of dozens of witnesses in Nuremberg and at the German embassy in Buenos Aires. A number of arrest warrants were issued in the case concerning the murder of the German citizen Elisabeth Käsemann in May 1977, including a warrant issued in November 2003 against the former president and military dictator Jorge Rafael Videla. The GDR *Politbüro* precedents were relied upon to argue that Videla could be held liable as commander of repressive military and state institutions and therefore tried as an indirect perpetrator of murder on the basis of the doctrine of *"mittelbare Täterschaft kraft Organisationsherrschaft"*. The German state then took up the case, attempting for many years to secure Videla's extradition. This work by the German judiciary can be seen in the context of the above-mentioned civil society strategy to overcome impunity for the crimes of the dictatorship in Argentina and can be considered to have made a crucial contribution to the success of July 2011, when the first convictions were handed down in Argentina for crimes that included Käsemann's murder.[2] In a similar case in respect of dictatorship crimes in Chile, prosecution authorities in Krefeld in the summer of 2011 opened proceedings against a leading member of the Colonia Dignidad sect for his part in decades of child abuse and for aiding the crimes of the Pinochet dictatorship, in particular the torture and enforced disappearance of opponents of the regime.

For the Argentine cases, the German prosecutors had to rely on the limited domestic criminal provisions available at the time which did not include specific provisions for crimes against humanity, torture and enforced disappearance. These crimes, together with war crimes and genocide – the other core international crimes – were later expressly incorporated into German law with the coming into force of the *Völkerstrafgesetzbuch* ('VStGB', German Code of Crimes against International Law)

---

[2]   On the German investigations into the crimes of the Argentine military, see Wolfgang Kaleck, *Kampf gegen die Straflosigkeit: Argentiniens Militärs vor Gericht*, Verlag Klaus Wagenbach, Berlin, 2010.

on 30 June 2002. The new code brought Germany's criminal laws in line with international standards and its state obligations under both long-standing customary international law and the ICC Statute. The introduction of the new code by Germany was motivated by a desire to contribute to the transnational prosecution of international crimes and thus support the work of the ICC, a body much championed by Germany.

The new laws were drafted to facilitate the prosecution of crimes against international law occurring after June 2002, even if committed outside of Germany by non-Germans and against non-Germans. Yet the initial hopes held by human rights organizations that Germany would, like Belgium and Spain, begin to enthusiastically investigate crimes committed abroad were soon dashed. Some of these expectations may in any case not have been very realistic, as evidenced by dozens of poorly constructed criminal complaints in respect of human rights violations submitted in various countries. At first, it also was a real problem that, unlike in other European states such as the Netherlands and the Scandinavian countries, Germany had not established a prosecution unit dedicated to investigating crimes against international law. This shortcoming was remedied in the late 2000s by centralizing prosecutions under the VStGB at the Office of the German Federal Prosecutor. No prosecutions were pursued under the VStGB between 2002 and 2008, partly due to the discussed deficiencies and partly because the focus of the authorities' efforts lay in other fields, such as the prosecution of crimes related to terrorism.

The Office of the Federal Prosecutor failed to initiate proceedings against the former Uzbek interior minister Zokirjon Almatov, despite the fact that he was present in Germany for medical treatment in the autumn of 2005. On learning of his presence in Germany, human rights organizations lodged criminal complaints against Almatov for crimes against humanity and torture. UN reports confirm Uzbekistan's notorious reputation for torture; it is reported that dissidents were even brutally tortured in the basement of the interior ministry. Almatov is also one of the main suspects in the Andijan massacre in May 2005 in which over 1,000 predominantly Muslim demonstrators were murdered. In light of these reports, the European Union added Almatov to a list of persons with a travel ban. Yet during his stay in Germany, for which an exception to the travel ban was granted, no steps were taken to pursue his prosecution. The proceedings were discontinued after he had left Germany on the basis that it would not be possible to complete the case in the absence of the suspect. While the exact details behind remain unclear – federal prosecution authorities claim they did not learn of Almatov's visit until it was too late, despite it being known to other ministries – the incident shows that prosecutions in high-profile cases are often blocked by political considerations. At the time, Uzbekistan was an important political ally due to its air base at Termez being used by the German military in its operations in Afghanistan.

In light of this assessment, the decision of the German authorities to discontinue investigations against Donald Rumsfeld and other US military and political figures in relation to the systematic torture in Abu Ghraib and Guantánamo is perhaps less surprising.

It took a long time before the first indictment trial on the basis of the VStGB occurred at the Higher Regional Court in Stuttgart. In May 2011 proceedings began against Ignace Murwanashyaka and Straton Musoni, two Hutu leaders residing in Germany who were charged on counts of crimes against humanity and war crimes. They are accused of having ordered massacres and rape by units of the Forces Démocratiques de Libération du Rwanda ('FDLR') in eastern Congo or at least to be criminally liable for these acts under the doctrine of command responsibility. The trial is expected to end with a judgment in the summer of 2015.

This case, like the trial of Onesphore Rwabukombe, a former Hutu mayor who was convicted and sentenced to 14 years in prison by the Higher Regional Court in Frankfurt for his role in the genocide in Rwanda in April 1994, shows the direction investigations by the Office of the German Federal Prosecutor are taking.

The Office of the Federal Prosecutor showed much less interest in pursuing investigations and prosecutions in the first case against a German citizen under the VStGB that concerned the German army colonel Georg Klein. The proceedings in respect of civilian casualties from an aerial bombing near Kunduz in Afghanistan in September 2009 were discontinued in the spring of 2010 after a brief and inadequate investigation which failed to even establish the number of civilian deaths. A constitutional complaint against the decision to discontinue the investigations which was lodged on behalf of victims and relatives is still pending before the Federal Constitutional Court.[3]

---

[3]　See Wolfgang Kaleck, Andreas Schüller and Dominik Steiger, "Tarnen und Täuschen – die deutschen Strafverfolgungsbehörden und der Fall des Luftangriffs bei Kundus", in *Kritische Justiz*, 2010, vol. 43, no. 3, pp. 270–286.

The Office of the Federal Prosecutor was equally quick to discontinue investigations into a US drone strike that killed the German citizen Bünyamin E. in Waziristan, Pakistan in October 2010, on the spurious grounds that the killing was justified under international humanitarian law.

In a more positive development, German federal prosecutors have started to monitor situations around the world in which international crimes have occurred even in cases where there is no direct link between the crime and Germany such as the presence of a suspect on German territory. These monitoring activities have been termed anticipative legal assistance – they aim at securing accessible evidence in order to be able to support proceedings which may be initiated abroad, in Germany or before the ICC at a later point in time. In the course of monitoring activities in respect of suspected war crimes and crimes against humanity committed by unidentified individuals during the civil war in Syria, testimony from more than two dozen witnesses now living in Germany has been gathered. Similar activities have been carried out in respect of war crimes committed during the Sri Lankan civil war and other situations.

8

Transnational Corporations and
International Criminal Law

When facing the prospect of international criminal investigations, it is not just political powers who seek to intervene. National and transnational corporations are often part of the power structures at the heart of dictatorships and conflict. Due to their status as non-state actors, corporations are for the most part not subjects of international law, so proceedings in connection with corporate crimes are rare and tend to be limited to criminal cases against specific responsible individuals such as arms dealers or company executives.

At the International Military Tribunal in Nuremberg, there had been plans to carry out further proceedings against corporations such as the Krupp group to demonstrate that there had been a military, economic and political conspiracy to launch a war of aggression. While ultimately this trial did not take place, a significant number of the 13 successor trials were directed against German firms (Krupp, Flick, IG Farben as well as the case against Röchling in Rastatt). In the view of the prosecutors in Nuremberg, the industrialists and financiers of the Hitler regime were no less dangerous than the German militarists, the SS officers or the leaders of the Nationalsozialistische Deutsche Arbeiterpartei (Nazi Party).[1] At the trials of the industrialists Flick and Krupp and the managers of IG Farben, the court undertook a detailed examination of the individual criminal liability of company executives in decisions that have since been relied on as precedents by lawyers around the world.[2] The defence arguments put forward in these cases give a preview of the kind of legal topos that remains the subject of much controversy to this day. In an expert opinion written on behalf of Friedrich Flick, Carl Schmitt argued that the defen-

---

[1] Quoted in the epilogue by the editor Helmut Quaritsch of Carl Schmitt, *Das international-rechtliche Verbrechen des Angriffskriegs und der Grundsatz "Nullum crimen, nulla poena sine lege"*, Duncker und Humblot, Berlin, 1994, p. 127.

[2] The major industrialist Friedrich Flick was convicted on 22 December 1947 of war crimes and crimes against humanity through the use of forced labour and concentration camp workers. He was sentenced to seven years' imprisonment, of which he served three (Case V).

dant was simply an "ordinary businessman", a citizen who was not involved in the commission of atrocities or in the inner workings of the regime, but who simply pursued what at the time were legitimate business dealings.[3]

In the period following the Nuremberg successor trials, hardly any further criminal proceedings were initiated against perpetrators of corporate crimes. No action was taken even in cases where companies were suspected of colluding with and profiting from dictatorships, where money was earned from both sides of a conflict and raw materials purchased that had been produced under inhumane conditions.

The most significant exceptions were the US compensation claims under the Alien Tort Claims Act mentioned earlier. Two important claims ended with settlements very favourable to the claimants and saw the respondent oil companies Unocal and Shell paying out multimillion-dollar sums to victims. The case against Unocal was initiated in 1996 and accused the company of building a pipeline with the help of forced labourers recruited by the Burmese military dictatorship. The Dutch firm Shell was sued in the USA in 1998 by members of the Ogoni people, including the family of murdered oppositionist Ken Saro Wiwa, for co-operating with the Nigerian military in the brutal repression of indigenous protests in the course of the company's operations in the Niger Delta. In one of the two cases, Shell agreed to pay an out-of-court settlement. The other case, Kiobel versus Shell, was decided by the US Supreme Court in April 2013. The ruling, which came as a severe blow to the victims and to human rights activists around the world, held that civil courts in the USA only have jurisdiction in cases of grave human rights violations where the case has a tangible link to the USA. This finding is ominous for other civil suits currently pending. The case of Sarei versus Rio Tinto that concerned the company's involvement in genocide and war crimes on the island of Bougainville in Papua New Guinea during the 1980s and 1990s was dismissed in June 2013 on the basis of the Kiobel decision.

Few such cases have been litigated in Europe. Along with some successful claims against British firms in environmental cases, the two most significant cases were heard in the Netherlands. Dutch courts convicted businessman Frans van Anraat of selling poison gas to Saddam Hussein, who used them in the massacres of Kurdish people in northern

---

[3]   Schmitt, 1994, p. 80, see *supra* note 1.

Iraq. The arms dealer Guus Kouwenhoven was charged with aiding war crimes and crimes against humanity in Liberia under Charles Taylor with no final decision having been reached yet.

Even in Argentina, a country that has led the way for legal proceedings into crimes against humanity, corporate actors suspected of dictatorship crimes have mostly managed to escape criminal prosecution. The current proceedings in Argentina have failed to address the corporations who were responsible for or at least contributed to the enforced disappearance of trade unionists and labour council members. This is despite the fact that the persecution of the organized labour movement was one of the key objectives of the Argentine military dictatorship. Key cases here are those taken against motor firms Ford and Mercedes Benz. Despite the presentation of numerous criminal complaints, extensive evidence and numerous witnesses, investigations into these cases have remained quite stagnant. Some progress, however, is on the horizon in the Ford case, where formal proceedings are now due to be taken up against three former managers of the company.

At first it seemed as if progress was being made on another significant case against corporate involvement in the crimes of the last military dictatorship. In August 2013 charges were levelled against the former owner and the former managing director of Argentine agribusiness firm Ledesma in Jujuy for their roles in human rights violations committed by the military regime. However, in early 2015 the Argentine Federal Criminal Cassation Court dropped the charges against the former owner for lack of evidence. If this decision, which has been strongly criticized by human rights groups, is confirmed on appeal, it would demonstrate that even nowadays corporate actors do not have to fear prosecution for crimes they have committed during the dictatorship.

Investigating the role of economic actors in these crimes is about more than simply securing individual prosecutions. It also helps to identify the structures and systematic conditions that foster, encourage or profit from crimes against international law. These facts can help to recognize the social and economic root causes of human rights violations and to draw the right conclusions in order to prevent such crimes in the future. As things stand, however, economic power structures tend to remain relatively intact even in countries that have undergone radical transitions, while foreign companies sweep in promising to help rebuild the destroyed societies so that corporate impunity for the damage wreaked remains rife.

9

Africa Only? The Practice of the International Criminal Court to Date

The establishment of the International Criminal Court marked a major step forward in efforts to tackle the most severe crimes at a global level. None of the major Cold War powers welcomed the development, wary as they were of having limits imposed on their sovereignty, particularly in such delicate matters, and being unwilling to be held to international standards or to have their citizens sanctioned by an uncontrollable world court. At the international conference on the establishment of the court in the summer of 1998, Germany, Canada, Australia and other supporters of the court formed a so-called alliance of 'like-minded states' which faced opposition from the more sceptical world powers China, Russia, India and the USA. Experience garnered at the ex-Yugoslavia and Rwanda tribunals aided discussions, providing a framework on which the new court could be based.

The conference turned its attention to the new court's jurisdiction and competence and to determining when and at whose initiative it would be able to initiate proceedings. The most far-reaching suggestion envisaged an independent court that was free to take up investigations as it saw fit under the principle of universal jurisdiction, regardless of where the crimes were committed and the nationality of the suspect or victim. A counter suggestion provided for a court that was permanent, but that could only act when authorized by the UN Security Council, an arrangement which would have allowed the veto powers to block any legal action unfavourable to themselves or their allies. Ultimately, a compromise was reached and set out in the ICC Statute, giving the court the power to launch investigations only into crimes committed on the territory of or by a national of one of the states party to the statute. The prosecutor is free to undertake investigations *proprio motu*, that is, on his or her own initiative subject to authorization by a pre-trial chamber of the court. The statute was adopted by an overwhelming majority at the conference, with only the USA, China, Israel, Iraq, Libya, Yemen and Qatar voting against. Russia, India and Iran joined the countries signing the statute, but have subsequently failed to ratify it. Despite concerted efforts by the USA to thwart its progress, the project was generally seen as a success, with the swift ratification process, the establishment of the ICC in The Hague on the statute's entry into force on 1 July 2002, and the continuously rising number of state parties (123 as of April 2015, including almost all European and Latin American states as well as many African states).

The court currently has jurisdiction in cases of genocide, crimes against humanity and war crimes. At the first Review Conference of the ICC Statute in 2010 in Kampala, Uganda, delegates worked on a proposal for the definition of the crime of aggression, which had been provisionally included in the original statute, but had its efficacy postponed until agreement could be reached on the content of the crime. The definition ultimately agreed upon does not encompass all uses of violence deemed illegal under the UN Charter, but includes only the most grave and clear instances of aggression. According to the procedure laid down in Kampala, the ICC should have the capacity to prosecute for crimes of aggression in limited circumstances by 2017.[1]

The territorial restrictions on the jurisdiction of the ICC mean that the veto powers, China, Russia and the USA, as well as other prominent non-party states including India, Indonesia and Iran remain outside the court's remit. Until recently, the same applied with regard to the non-member state of Israel, but since Palestine has become a member of the ICC Statute in early 2015, the court has jurisdiction with regard to crimes under the statute committed on Palestinian territory. This important development does not mean that there are no obstacles to an investigation of Israeli crimes by the ICC, as I discuss below. In 2000, towards the end of Bill Clinton's tenure as president, the USA signed the statute, but the move was subsequently revoked under President George W. Bush.[2] The USA had been closely involved in the early stages of the court's devel-

---

[1]   See Kai Ambos, "Das Verbrechen der Aggression nach Kampala", in *Zeitschrift für Internationale Strafrechtsdogmatik*, 2010, vol. 5, no. 11, pp. 649–668.

[2]   In 2002 the Bush administration took a hostile position towards the ICC with the signing into law of the American Servicemembers' Protection Act, allowing the USA to intervene – including with the use of military force – to secure the release of American citizens detained by or for the ICC. Slightly softening its boycott of the Court, the USA did however abstain from the 2005 UN Security Council vote on referring the situation in Darfur to the ICC, thus allowing the Court to take up the case. Under President Obama, the USA participated in the state party conferences as an observer, contributing suggestions on the crime of aggression at the Review Conference in Kampala in 2010.

opment and had long maintained hopes of a more dominant role for the UN Security Council. The refusal of many powerful states and regions to subject themselves to the court's jurisdiction goes some way to explain why the court's eight formal investigations to date have been limited to African states, namely Kenya, Uganda, Sudan, the Central African Republic, DR Congo, Libya, Mali and Côte d'Ivoire. This regional imbalance necessarily occupies a central spot in any appraisal of the ICC's work over the past decade.

9.1. Democratic Republic of the Congo

The ICC's first formal investigation was launched on 23 June 2004 after the situation in the DR Congo was referred to the court by the Congolese government. The case concerns crimes against international law committed in the Ituri region in the east of the DR Congo, where a conflict has been underway between various armed groups and the Congolese army since around 1999. The militia leader, Thomas Lubanga Dyilo, from the Union des Patriotes Congolais ('UPC'), aligned with the Hena people, was arrested in March 2006 by Congolese authorities and extradited to The Hague. He thereby became the first individual to be held in the ICC's detention centre and to be convicted by the court. On 14 March 2012 Lubanga was found guilty of the recruitment and enlistment of child soldiers between September 2002 and August 2003, and on 10 July 2012 he was sentenced to 14 years' imprisonment. The sentencing, which was appealed by both the defendant and the prosecutor, was confirmed on appeal in December 2014.

Germain Katanga, an ethnic Ngiti and leader of the Forces de Résistance Patriotique d'Ituri, and Mathieu Ngudjolo Chui from the Lendu group, commander of the Front des Nationalistes et Intégrationnistes who had been fighting for other parties to the conflict, were arrested in 2007 and 2008 and brought to The Hague. Chui was acquitted in 2012 due to insufficient evidence to support the charges of war crimes and crimes against humanity filed against him; this decision has been confirmed on appeal in February 2015. On 7 March 2014 the court found Katanga guilty of aiding and abetting crimes against humanity and war crimes during the massacre in the village of Bogoro on 24 February 2003. He was acquitted of charges of sexual slavery, rape and the use of child soldiers.

The third investigation into the situation in Congo is focused on the FDLR, the rebel group of exiled Rwandans active in Kivu.[3]

In light of large-scale human rights violations, particularly in the Ituri region and in Kivu, many commentators have criticized the fact that to date the court has targeted only rebel leaders while making no effort to prosecute suspects from the Congolese army or the Congolese, Rwandan and Ugandan governments. Human Rights Watch and a UN expert panel[4] have accused prosecutors in The Hague of failing to fulfil their own mandate to pursue prosecutions of those bearing the greatest responsibility for crimes under the court's jurisdiction. They make the point that Uganda had a hand in crimes in Congo as the occupying power in Ituri between 1998 and 2003 and as financier and supporter of rebel groups. They also point out that Rwanda trained and aided the UPC from 2002 to 2003, while the Congolese government is implicated in the conflict in northern Kivu, with the former foreign and incumbent planning minister Antipas Mbusa Nyamwisi holding responsibility for the crimes of another rebel group. While four parties are involved in the conflict in Kivu, the investigations in The Hague concern only the FDLR.

A further criticism focuses on the fact that the UPC's Thomas Lubanga was charged only with conscripting and enlisting child soldiers, something which observers say is practised by almost every party to the conflict in the region. No charges were brought in connection with the more significant accusations of murder, torture and large-scale sexualized violence. The prosecution authorities argued that because the suspect was being detained awaiting trial, they wished to conduct a focused investigation free from the delays that would have arisen had they also pursued the other charges. The Lubanga trial was furthermore tainted by the Office of the Prosecutor's failure to forward to the defence certain relevant documents which it had obtained from the UN – a clear violation of due process.

Hence, the prosecution is being heavily criticized for inadequate and selective investigations with regard to the situation in the DR Congo.

---

3   Callixte Mbarushimana was arrested in France in October 2010 and extradited to The Hague. In December 2011 his case was discontinued owing to a lack of evidence. He was released in December 2011.

4   UN Panel of Experts on the Illegal Exploitation of Natural Resources and Other Forms of Wealth of the Democratic Republic of the Congo.

The limited number of investigations and absence of any discernable roadmap as to when and against whom further cases might be taken have led to a growing belief among local leaders, civil society representatives and foreign observers that the ICC lacks impartiality.[5] The ICC's maiden cases on the DR Congo have thus revealed how the horizontal and vertical selectivity of prosecutions can have a significant negative impact on the legitimacy and efficiency of the court in the entire affected region.

9.2. Uganda

This assessment is confirmed by the investigations concerning Uganda, a party to the ICC Statute and one of the court's most important allies in Africa. In 2004 President Yoweri Museveni referred to the jurisdiction of the ICC the 20-year armed conflict in northern Uganda and the crimes of the Lord's Resistance Army ('LRA') on the basis that the government did not consider itself in a position to end the LRA's ongoing violence, let alone to bring the perpetrators to trial. Following investigations, the ICC issued arrest warrants against the five LRA leaders Joseph Kony, Okot Odhiambo, Dominic Ongwen, Vincent Otti und Raska Lukwiya. It has not been possible to secure arrests in these cases as some have died or are reported dead while the surviving suspects remain at large. The only exception is Ongwen who had himself been conscripted as a child soldier and surrendered to the ICC after more than 25 years in the LRA in early 2015. The violence carried out in more recent years by the LRA in the border region between northern Uganda, DR Congo and South Sudan, some of it led by a new generation of LRA commanders, is not yet under investigation in The Hague.

Once again the court has been criticized for focusing its investigations on just one party to the conflict, the LRA, while ignoring crimes committed by the Ugandan army. The ICC's prosecutor at the time justified this by pointing out that the crimes of the Ugandan army were of a smaller scale.[6] Human rights organizations demand that the prosecutor

---

[5] Human Rights Watch, *Unfinished Business: Closing Gaps in the Selection of ICC Cases*, Human Rights Watch, New York, 2011, pp. 9 ff., available at http://www.hrw.org/sites/default/files/reports/icc0911webwcover.pdf, last accessed on 29 March 2015.

[6] International Federation for Human Rights, *ICC: The International Criminal Court's First Years*, Fédération internationale des ligues des droits de l'Homme, Paris, 2009, p. 9, available at https://www.fidh.org/IMG/pdf/NoteCPI516anglais2009.pdf, last accessed on 29 March 2015.

provide at least a rudimentary justification for such decisions in order to improve transparency, combat the claims of bias, and clear the way for domestic criminal proceedings in Uganda.[7]

Furthermore, the fundamental debate on peace versus justice has a bearing on the Uganda situation. At its core is the question whether the work of the ICC can actually fuel conflicts and stand in the way of peace negotiations. In the case of Uganda the facts are uncertain. It is claimed that the court's investigations prompted the LRA to pull out of promising peace negotiations with the Ugandan government as it feared prosecution and the arrest of its leaders. Others say that the ICC's work should be credited with having caused the LRA to enter into peace talks in the first place and that the prosecutors' work helped to ease the violence.[8] In almost all of the situations discussed in this chapter, claims were made by the suspects and sympathetic intellectuals as well as some legal and political science scholars that the ICC proceedings were leading to unrest, chaos and civil war and hindered the reconciliation needed within the affected societies. Such claims remain without any factual corroboration. It is worth noting that, in hindsight, warnings against prosecutions almost always prove unjustified. Recent research indicates that subjecting criminal regimes to the rule of law tends to advance human rights standards; predictions of outbreaks of violence on account of criminal proceedings have not come to pass. What emerges is that these kinds of concerns are often raised by those with a vested interest in ensuring that prosecutions do not take place.

9.3. Darfur, Sudan

The situation in Darfur was referred to the ICC by the UN Security Council in March 2005. On 6 June of that year the Office of the Prosecutor in The Hague opened formal proceedings against the sitting Sudanese president Omar Hassan al-Bashir, the former minister Ahmad Muhammad Harun (Ali Kushyab) and the leader of the Janjaweed militia, Ali Muhammad Ali Abd-Al-Rahman.

---

[7]   Human Rights Watch, 2011, pp. 23 ff., see *supra* note 5.

[8]   International Federation for Human Rights, 2009, see *supra* note 6; Makau Mutua, *The International Criminal Court in Africa*, Norwegian Peacebuilding Centre, Working Paper, September 2010, p. 4, available at http://www.peacebuilding.no/var/ezflow_site/storage/ original/application/d5dc6870a40b79bf7c1304f3befe0b55.pdf, last accessed on 29 March 2015.

Sudan has not signed the ICC Statute and refuses to co-operate with the court. While the court issued arrest warrants for Ali Kushyab in 2007 and al-Bashir in 2009, without any assistance from Sudan both suspects remain at large. The prosecution's pursuit of al-Bashir has been the subject of great controversy, with critics claiming that the arrest warrant has hindered the much more important process of finding a way to peacefully resolve the conflict.[9]

That no arrest could be secured following the ICC's first-ever arrest warrant for a sitting head of state has been interpreted as an indication of the weakness of the court. In fact, there were a number of other factors at play. The UN Security Council failed to provide sufficient support to the court after it had made its referral. No sanctions were taken against Sudan to force the state to co-operate with the court and no action was taken by the Security Council against the states that hosted state visits by al-Bashir, including state parties to the ICC Statute (Djibouti, Chad, Libya, Malawi and Kenya).[10] In the face of these obstacles, the ICC's prosecutor Fatou Bensouda announced in December 2014 that she would suspend investigations into the Darfur situation due to a lack of support by the Security Council.

9.4. Further Investigations

In December 2004 the Central African Republic, an ICC state party, called on the court to open investigations into crimes committed during the armed conflict on its territory in 2002 and 2003. The court's investiga-

---

[9] Critics also argued that the Court's issuance of the arrest warrant served only to create the impression that the Court was taking action. Furthermore, they felt it was wrong of the Court to include a charge of genocide instead of limiting the charges to war crimes and crimes against humanity as it would be extremely difficult to prove there was the intent to destroy the repressed Fur, Masalit and Zaghawa ethnic groups. Difficult legal issues led to a nine-month delay in issuing the warrant for crimes against humanity. An arrest warrant for genocide was issued in July 2010.

[10] In a report from September 2011 Human Rights Watch is critical of the investigation's failure to include other senior members of the government and military. They point to the continued absence of a coherent strategy on the part of the prosecution to prosecute those most responsible for the genocide in Darfur. While – as in the situations in DR Congo and Uganda – there is little doubt that grave crimes were committed over a protracted period of time, the prosecution faces widespread criticism of the political selectivity as well as of the choice of defendants and the focus of individual charges. See Human Rights Watch, "World Report 2011: Sudan", available at http://www.hrw.org/world-report-2011/sudan, last accessed on 7 May 2015.

tions eventually led to the arrest of the Congolese militia leader and former vice president, Jean-Pierre Bemba. He is accused of committing or commanding crimes against humanity, including the mass rape of men, women and children. Once again the arrest prompted accusations of selectivity. Commentators argued that Bemba was being singled out as a scapegoat and that his removal from the political landscape was particularly convenient for many in the Central African Republic and in particular for Joseph Kabila's Congolese government.[11] The court's failure to investigate crimes committed by troops belonging to François Bozizé, who served as head of government of the Central African Republic until he was ousted by the rebel group Séléka in March 2013, and the unsatisfactory reasons provided for this, have done little to alleviate suspicions of bias on the part of the court.[12]

In Kenya, elections in December 2007 gave rise to violent clashes over the course of which more than 1,000 people were killed, 3,500 seriously injured and up to 650,000 displaced from their homes, crimes for which the police, security forces and militias were blamed. The violence subsided following an intervention of the international community, but efforts to bring those responsible to justice in Kenyan courts proved unsuccessful. The ICC's prosecutor at the time decided to initiate proceedings in the case with regard to crimes against humanity, the first time it had used its powers to open an investigation of its own accord. The investigation focused on six high-ranking political actors, including the former minister for finance Uhuru Kenyatta, who was elected president in March 2013, and William Ruto who acts as his vice president. During trial, special arrangements largely exempted Ruto, Kenyatta and the head of operations of Kenyan radio station Kass FM, Joshua Arap Sang, from the obligation to be present in The Hague. Sang and Ruto are still standing trial, but the charges against Kenyatta were withdrawn by the prosecution in December 2014 for a lack of evidence which, according to Bensouda's office, was mostly due to a Kenyan refusal to co-operate during investigations. The three other proceedings had earlier been discontinued, too. The Kenyan cases have been a cause for debate even among the judges at the court, some of whom had doubts as to whether the events in Kenya reached the threshold of crimes against humanity. This is a common prob-

---

[11]   Mutua, 2010, p. 5 f., see *supra* note 8.
[12]   Human Rights Watch, 2011, pp. 31 ff., see *supra* note 5.

lem that arises in situations – often in the context of elections – where opposing political groups clash, leading to protests and escalation in violence.

A similar scenario unfolded in Côte d'Ivoire where large-scale violence broke out following elections. In May 2011 the ICC's prosecutor at the time, Luis Moreno Ocampo, opened investigations concerning the ousted former president Laurent Gbagbo at the behest of the new president Alassane Ouattara. Gbagbo was extradited to The Hague, where he is jointly with his former aide Charles Blé Goudé awaiting the commencement of their trial.

Furthermore, in January 2013 ICC prosecution authorities launched formal investigations into crimes that occurred after January 2012 during the armed conflict in northern Mali, a state party to the ICC Statute. Cases against specific individuals have not yet been initiated.

9.5. Libya

As the Arab Spring revolts began to spill over into Libya in early 2011, its leaders turned to military measures to quell the protests. The violence was at its worst in Benghazi and al-Bayda, where hundreds of civilian demonstrators were killed and injured while thousands more, mostly dissidents, were made to disappear by the Gaddafi regime. Cluster bombs and other military weapons were deployed against the civilian population in Misrata. In March 2011 Resolution 1970 was passed by the UN Security Council, referring the situation to the ICC under Article 13(b) of the ICC Statute in what was – owing to the support of the USA – the first unanimous referral of a case to the court. Prosecution authorities immediately began investigations, issuing an arrest warrant for the Libyan leader Muammar Gaddafi and his son, Saif Al-Islam Gaddafi, as well as the head of the military intelligence service, Abdullah Al-Senussi, in connection with crimes against humanity. The African Court on Human Rights and the African Commission on Human Rights both issued decisions in spring 2011, describing the situation in Libya as extremely serious and qualifying the human rights violations as widespread and systematic. Amnesty International also issued several reports on human rights violations committed by the insurgents who fought back against the regime's repression (arbitrary arrest, extrajudicial execution, lynching and torture). The rebels predominantly targeted sub-Saharan Africans and black Libyans, based on a prejudiced belief that black soldiers worked as mercenaries for the Gaddafi government.[13]

Yet again, the ICC's actions gave rise to a debate on the impartiality of the court after NATO forces who had been intervening in Libya were granted immunity from prosecution before the ICC, despite evidence of numerous civilian deaths caused by NATO airstrikes. Thus, a representative of Human Rights Watch felt prompted to criticize the prevailing "atmosphere of impunity".[14]

The proceedings against Muammar Gaddafi were discontinued after his death in November 2011. The court also declared the case against Al-Senussi inadmissible since Libya is both willing and able to carry out genuine prosecution. The ICC is still waiting for Saif Gaddafi to be extradited and therefore issued a finding of non-compliance against Libya in December 2014. His transfer to The Hague seems ever more unlikely, as Libya has become entangled in an escalating factional armed conflict since early 2014.

9.6. Monitoring

The prosecution authorities at the ICC have set up an analysis unit to monitor and conduct preliminary reviews of situations around the world that might warrant further investigation.[15] The prosecutors can also take up investigations in response to third-party requests. As of 31 December 2013, 10,470 communications – similar to a criminal complaint – had been submitted to the court by victims, governments and human rights organizations. The court has announced preliminary investigations into situations in Afghanistan (including potential NATO crimes), Colombia, Georgia, Nigeria, Honduras, South Korea, the Comoros, the Central African Republic, Ukraine and Guinea.

---

[13] See Amnesty International, *Detention Abuses Staining the New Libya*, Amnesty International, London, 2011, p. 8, available at https://www.amnesty.org/en/documents/MDE19/036/2011/en/, last accessed on 29 March 2015.

[14] Quoted in Christopher J. Chivers and Eric Schmitt, "In Strikes on Libya by NATO, an Unspoken Civilian Toll", in *The New York Times*, 17 December 2011.

[15] See Human Rights Watch, "Course Correction: Recommendations to the ICC Prosecutor for a More Effective Approach to 'Situations under Analysis'", June 2011, available at http://www.hrw.org/sites/default/files/related_material/HRW%20Course%20Correction_0.pdf, last accessed on 30 March 2015.

The court's preliminary examinations and its publicly announced monitoring of situations increase the pressure on the countries in question to carry out their own investigations, an effect that could be described as 'positive complementarity'. This kind of monitoring can also have a preventive function. The problem, however, is the lack of uniformity in the prosecution's approach. The preliminary examination concerning Colombia has dragged on for a long time with no fixed timeframe and insufficient pressure being exerted, whereas the court consistently urges the national prosecution authorities to take investigatory action and to make arrests in other contexts, for example in Kenya and Guinea.

9.7. The Case of Colombia

The Office of the Prosecutor in The Hague has been monitoring the situation in Colombia since 2006. The most noteworthy investigations to date have centred on accusations against Colombian paramilitaries and the politicians close to them.

There is a general consensus that war crimes and crimes against humanity were committed in Colombia, a state party to the ICC Statute, both before and after the coming into force of the ICC Statute in 2002.[16] The ICC could therefore take up formal proceedings, but only as long as no competing proceedings are underway in Colombian courts. This caveat is due to Article 17 of the ICC Statute which lays down the principle of complementarity. This provision ensures that domestic proceedings have priority, as it declares ICC proceedings inadmissible whenever the state in question is willing and able to conduct these to an adequate standard itself. Inability to conduct proceedings might occur in the case of the complete or partial collapse of a judicial system. The issue of unwillingness is much more difficult to judge in a case where the state takes the requisite legislative and judicial steps towards prosecution, thereby creating the impression that it is fulfilling its legal obligations, when in fact no genuine efforts to prosecute are made. That the requisite will to pursue proceedings is indeed absent in Colombia is indicated by widespread attempts to protect suspects from prosecution, undue delays and a lack of independence and impartiality on the part of the prosecution authorities.

---

[16] See, in general, Kai Ambos, *The Colombian Peace Process and the Principle of Complementarity of the International Criminal Court*, Springer, Heidelberg, 2010.

Following the (partial) demobilization of the paramilitaries, Colombia passed Law 975 in 2005 which paved the way for the prosecution of sections of the paramilitaries. Under this law, suspects can benefit from a reduced sentence if they co-operate during trial. While 300,000 victims of human rights violations have been registered as part of the process towards accountability for crimes committed by the paramilitaries,[17] many of which predate Colombia's signing of the ICC Statute in November 2002, proceedings have been launched against only around 10 per cent of the estimated 30,000 paramilitary suspects. According to the Human Rights Watch World Report 2014, Colombian courts had convicted just 18 paramilitaries by July 2013, with only a minority of these actively co-operating with the court. While some progress has been made, the fact that 90 per cent of the paramilitaries have avoided prosecution, coupled with ongoing efforts to set down in law what had become a *de facto* amnesty, point undeniably to the conclusion that an atmosphere of impunity persists in Colombia. Particularly discouraging is the continuing failure to prosecute senior military commanders and key figures from politics and industry who were closely connected with the paramilitaries. In view of these deficiencies, critics call for a prosecution strategy with a greater focus on the senior figures within the political and (para)military leadership. This objective was greatly hindered by Colombia's decision to extradite 14 senior paramilitaries to the USA in connection with drug offences. Some of the individuals extradited had just begun to give evidence against certain politicians in a number of private and public hearings in Colombia which led to the initiation of investigations against around a third of the members of congress. The extraditions were overseen by the then president Álvaro Uribe Vélez, who is among those suspected of collaborating with the paramilitaries, without securing written assurances from the USA that Colombian prosecutors would continue to have access to the extradited suspects. The extradition thus essentially blocked any further participation of the suspects in the Colombian investigations. Since they were planning to give evidence against high-ranking figures who planned and ordered crimes, the paramilitaries understandably requested protection for their families, protection that the state failed to adequately guarantee.

---

[17] *Ibid.*, p. 52. Ambos writes of around 95,000 deaths between 1964 and 2007 arising from the armed conflict, from between 3 and 4.6 million internally displaced persons, over 7,000 disappeared persons, and an alarmingly high number of victims of torture.

Since 2009, however, the Colombian Supreme Court and state prosecutors have opened 83 proceedings against members of congress and a number of other state officials in connection with a case known as the 'parapolitics' scandal; at least 55 officials have thus far been convicted on account of their links with the paramilitaries. In 2013 preliminary investigations into links between Uribe and paramilitaries were opened, and Uribe's former security chief Mauricio Santoyo was formally named as a suspect with regard to the forced disappearances of two human rights activists in 2000. Notwithstanding, these minor successes do not justify the ICC's failure to act on the case, particularly given that there are no plans in the short or medium term for further action in Colombia and that the Office of the Prosecutor in The Hague has been monitoring the situation for roughly 10 years without opening formal proceedings. In the autumn of 2012, my own organization, ECCHR, submitted a criminal complaint to the ICC concerning the widespread repression of Colombian trade unions and the murder of a number of trade unionists. The opening of a formal investigation by the ICC would have the potential to trigger significant progress within Colombia in terms of accountability for international crimes.

9.8. Great Britain: Torture in Iraq

There has been much criticism for the court's handling of criminal complaints against Tony Blair and other British citizens in connection with war crimes committed during the war in Iraq from 2003 onwards. A complaint submitted to the Office of the Prosecutor by an international group of professors focused on torture and the use of cluster bombs by British forces in and around Basra as well as on allegations of war crimes in the context of detainee abuse.[18] They argue that the use of cluster ammunitions in urban areas represents war crimes due to the intentional infliction of disproportionate civilian casualties although these weapons are not banned as such. In a letter to those who submitted communications on the issue that was published in 2006, the prosecutor Moreno Ocampo said prosecutions had not been opened as the crimes denounced were not of sufficient gravity to fall within the jurisdiction of the ICC. Without undertaking any further inquiries, the prosecution assumed that the denounced

---

[18] See Bill Bowring, *The Degradation of the International Legal Order? The Rehabilitation of Law and the Possibility of Politics*, Routledge-Cavendish, Abingdon, 2008, pp. 64 ff.

prisoner abuse involved a relatively small number (12 to 14) of victims and argued that the incidents were of minor gravity in comparison with the ongoing investigations into crimes in Darfur, DR Congo and Rwanda. The letter also argued that the crimes were not part of a plan or policy, which under Article 8(1) of the ICC Statute is a consideration to take into account in establishing the court's jurisdiction in cases of war crimes.

Moreno Ocampo is to be criticized for failing to further investigate and thus massively underestimating the true dimensions of British war crimes in Iraq. Following the British internal Baha Mousa inquiry and the more recent decisions against Britain by the European Court of Human Rights, which found the UK to be in violation of its obligations to investigate such cases,[19] there should no longer be any doubt that the abuse of detainees in Iraq, including by British forces, occurred on a much wider scale than officially disclosed.

In January 2014 the British law firm Public Interest Lawyers ('PIL') and ECCHR submitted a joint submission to the ICC concerning the systematic torture and abuse of prisoners under British control between the invasion in 2003 and the end of the occupation in 2008. The complaint called on the court to launch investigations into the role of senior members of the British military as well as former ministers and state secretaries. Over the past years, over 400 former Iraqi prisoners have come forward to detail grave abuse and degrading treatment at the hands of British soldiers to PIL. The 250-page complaint focuses on 85 representative cases encompassing more than 2,000 individual claims of abuse across the period between 2003 and 2008 in various British detention centres. The document also includes relevant extracts from 41 witness testimonies, statements from the International Committee of the Red Cross, NGO and media reports as well as extensive evidence that emerged from various public inquiries in Britain.

While these official investigations have revealed the massive scope of the claims, British authorities failed to prosecute the vast majority of those involved. In particular, no efforts were made to establish the criminal liability of senior political and military figures for their roles as com-

---

[19] I refer to cases of European Court of Human Rights, *Al-Skeini and Others v. United Kingdom*, Application No. 55721/07, Judgment, 7 July 2011, and European Court of Human Rights, *Al-Jedda v. United Kingdom*, Application No. 27021/08, 7 July 2011. The applicants had been detained and abused by British forces in Iraq.

manders. In May 2014 the prosecution authorities in The Hague opened a preliminary examination in response to the additional information and evidence provided in the submission.

9.9. Outlook: The Next Ten Years

While the establishment of the court was initially greeted with great optimism and praise, many critical voices have emerged over the past 13 years.[20]

Although it is true that the eight formal proceedings opened by the court at the time of writing exclusively concern African countries, it is worth noting that two of these were referred to the court by the UN Security Council and four others were referred by the states in question themselves. Against this background, it becomes clear that accusations of bias or of a neocolonial or neoimperial attitude against the Office of the Prosecutor are only partially justified.

One very significant problem the ICC is facing is its limited scope to pursue cases. The court's investigations are very resource intensive and it is already reaching the limits of its capacity. The problem is exacerbated by its need to secure additional financing for any cases referred by the UN Security Council or by affected states. The fact that the ICC lacks its own executive – a problem that previously plagued the *ad hoc* tribunals as well – means that the court is highly dependent on the co-operation and support of states, particularly when it comes to transferring the suspects to The Hague. While investigations may be undertaken without the accused being present, the court is not permitted to carry out trials *in absentia*. Once an arrest warrant has been issued, access to the defendant depends on the willingness of the authorities in the individual's country of presence to extradite the suspect. As the case of al-Bashir demonstrates, such co-operation cannot always be guaranteed, even from state parties to the

---

[20] David Kaye sees the Court's record as nothing short of disastrous, "Who's Afraid of the International Criminal Court?", in *Foreign Affairs*, 2011, vol. 90, no. 3, pp. 118–129. He notes the former chief prosecutor Luis Moreno Ocampo's bold assertions that impunity has been eradicated from Libya, and compares this assessment with the reality of the Court's work to date: at that point no trial had been successfully completed, the two most prominent suspects (Sudanese president Omar al-Bashir and Joseph Kony, leader of the Ugandan rebel army the Lord's Resistance Army) remain at large despite the warrants for their arrest, and all of the Court's cases concern crimes committed in Africa, seriously undermining the Court's aspirations to act as a world court.

ICC Statute who are legally bound to fully co-operate with the court. During the investigation stage, the ICC is also reliant on assistance from other states, particularly from the states in which the crimes were committed, in order to gain access to witnesses and evidence. This kind of assistance, too, can generally only be counted on if the state in question feels that co-operating will in some way prove advantageous.

The court's jurisdiction extends only to crimes committed since July 2002 and is also subject to certain geographical limitations. There can be no doubt that the first three situations to be addressed by the ICC, which concerned the DR Congo, Darfur and Uganda, involved human rights violations on a massive scale. The issue becomes less clear in relation to the investigations with regard to Kenya, Côte d'Ivoire and Libya, all of which concern human rights violations which, in terms of duration, intensity and structure, are on a markedly smaller scale than the initial three. Situations of comparable gravity have occurred in a range of other settings, namely Burma, Chechnya, Colombia, Iran, Syria, Palestine and Sri Lanka. None of these countries, however, has signed the ICC Statute (with the exception of Colombia and, since early 2015, Palestine), and unlike Darfur and Libya, none of these situations has been referred to the court by the UN Security Council. Great power politics make a referral in these cases seem very unlikely, as at least one veto power has a stake in all of these situations.

The ICC's failure to move beyond monitoring the situation in Colombia and to initiate formal proceedings against what amounts to the most important ally of the USA in Latin America is the court's greatest shortcoming to date. While some efforts were carried out to pursue prosecutions within Colombia in a process that compares favourably to less successful attempts in Burma, Russia and Sri Lanka, the domestic proceedings remain far from satisfactory. The criticism that political selectivity was at play in the past in the case of British war crimes in Iraq is certainly warranted as well.

In spite of this assessment, there does seem, at least at first glance, to be a certain cogency about the prosecution's argument that the above-mentioned crimes lack the grand dimensions envisioned by the court's founders. It nonetheless represents an unsatisfactory state of affairs if possible war crimes committed by European states go unpunished merely because the ICC does not have the capacity to pursue such cases or because the crimes in questions are located on the fringes of the court's mandate. This is especially true where little or no legal action is taken in competent European courts.

The same charge of political selectivity should not yet be applied to the case of the Gaza war in light of the jurisdictional problems encountered by the court due to the long-lasting uncertainty surrounding Palestine's status as a state. This delicate question has, however, been resolved by the UN General Assembly when it recognized Palestine as a non-member observer state in November 2012. It followed that Palestine accepted the jurisdiction of the ICC with regard to "crimes within the jurisdiction of the Court committed in the occupied Palestinian territory, including East Jerusalem, since June 13, 2014" by virtue of an *ad hoc* declaration on 1 January 2015 and ratified the Statute on the following day. The Palestinian authorities seem to have chosen this bifurcated strategy, as the declaration of 1 January 2015 under Article 12(3) of the ICC Statute allowed them to trigger ICC jurisdiction by 13 June 2014. This is the day on which clashes began after the kidnapping of three Israeli teenagers which eventually led to the 2014 war in Gaza that lasted until the end of August and claimed 2,256 Palestinian and 85 Israeli lives. If Palestine had become a member state without such prior declaration, the court would only have had jurisdiction over crimes committed after the entry into force of the Statute for Palestine on 1 April 2015. On 16 January 2015 the ICC Office of the Prosecutor initiated a preliminary examination of the situation in Palestine. Needless to say, any investigation into Israeli suspects would probably expose the court to the staunchest political criticism by Israel and its Western allies and especially the USA. However, this is precisely why the court could now prove its independence by carrying out effective investigations into crimes committed by Israel and Hamas during the 2014 war. Past experience, for example with regard to British crimes in Iraq, suggests that there is some scope to hope for effective investigations, although the court will probably be slow to actively engage with this politically sensitive topic. NGO efforts could play a key role in keeping up pressure for the investigations to go ahead and in exposing any existing domestic unwillingness to investigate and prosecute.

In conclusion, it seems that it would be an oversimplification to argue that the ICC's focus on Africa up to the time of writing is solely due to the prejudice and interventionist approach of Western nations. It is an argument that has been seized upon by representatives of the African Union to denounce the court, for example, in the summer of 2011 after arrest warrants were issued for Gaddafi family members. They proposed the establishment of a court for Africa as an African solution to an African problem. This plan will be achieved by extending the jurisdiction of the African Court on Human and Peoples' Rights to criminal matters in its proposed new form as the African Court of Justice and Human Rights. In response, African human rights organizations correctly point out that African courts are already free to pursue their own prosecutions in these cases. Indeed, under the principle of complementarity their proceedings would have priority over those in The Hague. It therefore seems that charges of neocolonialism against the ICC have frequently been relied upon by African elites keen on deflecting pressure to bring to justice the perpetrators of severe human rights violations against African peoples. At the same time, the court has a long road ahead before its efforts can be considered untarnished by accusations of political selectivity.

10

The Future of Transnational Criminal Justice
and the Cosmopolitan Struggle for Human Rights

International criminal law, like criminal law in general, should neither be portrayed as the ideal nor as the only means of resolving social conflicts. By the time recourse can be had to the law, it is almost always too late to prevent human rights violations, which is one of the reasons why alternative responses to systemic injustice can be useful. Apart from criminal proceedings before national and international courts, other suggested pillars of transnational justice include truth commissions based on the South African model, various forms of material and immaterial compensation to the victims, public apologies, commemorations, and political reforms such as personnel changes within bureaucratic and security services.

A number of commentators consider criminal proceedings to be fundamentally ill-suited to dealing with systemic injustice and crimes directed by state institutions.[1] They point out that criminal proceedings focus on establishing the criminal liability of an individual person accused of violating a prohibitive norm, the validity of which, however, has often been suspended during the unjust regimes that frequently prevailed at the time of commission. Questions have also been raised as to how meaningful it is to pursue the punishment of individuals in the context of enormous crimes against humanity such as the Holocaust. International criminal law, it is argued, brings with it the risk of instrumentalizing criminal proceedings against individuals for broader political ends, such as an educational or a symbolic purpose. It was in this sense that Hannah Arendt, writing about Eichmann's trial in Jerusalem in 1961, famously branded the Israeli prime minister David Ben-Gurion the "invisible stage manager of the proceedings".[2] The question of the purpose of criminal punishment, highly controversial within the framework of national law, proves even more problematic in international criminal law. This is exacerbated by the

---

[1] See Mark A. Drumbl, *Atrocity, Punishment, and International Law*, Cambridge University Press, Cambridge, 2007.

[2] Hannah Arendt, *Eichmann in Jerusalem: A Report on the Banality of Evil*, Viking Press, New York, 1965, p. 5.

lack of consistent practice when it comes to prosecuting international crimes.

It remains the case that the likelihood of an individual facing prosecution for international crimes in the aftermath of a conflict situation is not very high. As such, the deterrent potential of the system is limited. Furthermore, in cases where the conflict in question has come to an end and a regime change has already taken place at the time of prosecution, there is little chance of recidivism, that is, of similar crimes being committed by the formerly powerful perpetrators, and a limited need for a specific deterrent effect on the perpetrators and their extended circles. Where the conflict is ongoing, it remains to be conclusively determined whether bringing criminal charges before an international court has a preventative effect on the commission of crimes. In fact, some claim it can have the opposite effect and cite the discussed case of Sudan or Uganda before the ICC as examples. Other authors argue that the increasingly common prosecution of international crimes does have an international deterrent effect, or at least influences behaviour, particularly in neighbouring regions or when potential perpetrators can identify with those individuals facing prosecution.[3]

According to the theory of positive general deterrence, punishment should serve a communicative purpose. The sentencing of an individual who broke a law should (re)affirm society's commitment to upholding the norm in question as well as its resolve to uphold the law in general. This can come about when an international or national institution considers and delivers a verdict on a given incident, characterizing it as an unjust act. If an accused, who had previously relied on violence to exert power, can be made to accept the code of right and wrong during the course of a criminal trial, the violence formerly committed is stripped of its communicative power and the accused is ultimately delegitimized by the legal proceedings.[4]

Prosecution before international courts is often questioned on the basis that the impact of such prosecution on the affected societies is too limited or in some cases even detrimental, and in any case not well

---

[3] See Kathryn Sikkink, *The Justice Cascade: How Human Rights Prosecutions Are Changing World Politics*, W.W. Norton, New York, 2011, pp. 129 ff.

[4] Jan Philipp Reemtsma, *Trust and Violence: An Essay on a Modern Relationship*, Princeton University Press, Princeton, NJ, 2012, pp. 276, 277.

enough understood.[5] It is argued that too little regard is had to cultural circles that are unfamiliar with Western criminal proceedings, and that the material and immaterial needs of the victims and their communities are not adequately taken into consideration. This very apt criticism poses a serious challenge to those who advocate using the criminal justice system to address past conflicts. It is no longer sufficient to argue in abstract terms or with abstract concepts. The task instead is to demonstrate why, based on past experience, criminal proceedings are – from more than a legal point of view – necessary and what impact they are likely to have. Positive effects worthy of mention are, for example, compensation of frequently traumatized victims and their communities, or changes in the way security forces conduct their activities. Past experience, for example in respect of Argentina, also shows that the various approaches are not mutually exclusive: a truth commission can be followed by a criminal trial, or a partial amnesty might precede comprehensive prosecutions.

My own position is a wholly level-headed and pragmatic one that takes into account the limits of criminal proceedings when it comes to dealing with past injustices. It should not be assumed that criminal proceedings are always advisable. In each particular case, reasons should be put forward to justify having recourse to criminal law procedures. This especially holds true for proceedings undertaken before international courts or those of third states.

10.1. Double Standards

The last two decades have seen human rights violations in virtually all regions of the world which have in various situations amounted to international crimes. And even where criminal prosecutions would be legally possible and indeed obligatory, the perpetrators of such crimes all too frequently continue to enjoy complete impunity. The reasons for this have been debated extensively. Conflict and post-conflict societies often lack functioning legal systems. Where state structures still exist or have been rebuilt, corruption, insufficient political will, an overburdened judiciary or divided societies coincide with a varying level of residual trauma as well as ongoing insecurity.

---

5   See, for example, Drumbl, 2007, *supra* note 1.

A consistent and universal response to international crimes in the form of legal consequences and sanctions was still absent at the end of the first decade of the 21st century. The obligations to investigate and prosecute genocide, crimes against humanity and torture that arise from various conventions and binding international law still lack enforcement.

In light of this lack of a standardized practice of international criminal justice, the question arises if it would be more pertinent to work towards establishing and developing such a practice first, before addressing the issue of existing double standards.

I think we can and indeed should pursue both aims simultaneously. Crucially, we can hardly speak about the global rule of law before the same law is applied to all. Apart from the fact that this kind of discriminatory application of norms is far removed from the concept of justice, a crucial element of criminal law is the expectation that violated norms will be restabilized by way of legal proceedings, that unjust acts will be characterized as such, and that violations of the law will be sanctioned. The current practice of prosecuting international crimes remains selective. Western states – those who generally lead the call for universal human rights and universal criminal prosecution – oppose prosecutions of their own crimes, or of their complicity in the crimes of other states. Scepticism has also grown over the last years in the Global South among states and non-state actors who would generally have been supportive of universal prosecution. This is in part due to the historical experiences of these societies, some of which have suffered for centuries under colonial and post-colonial repression, especially of an economic nature. Political and military actors, particularly those who themselves belong in the dock, know how to exploit this for their own benefit. Ignoring these attitudes and perceptions is dangerous.

We live in a global constellation in which the most powerful states only half-heartedly support the idea of international criminal justice. This kind of global political endeavour, however, requires the support not only of Western, but of African, Asian and Latin American states as well, in order to be successful. Hence, this issue deserves much more attention. It should concern everybody who strives for a radical change in global relations and works for a different, socially just world, as much as it is relevant to those who believe in the rule of law and who work towards the constitutionalization of global relations. A cause of worry for the latter group should be that adjudication could lose its legitimacy. Especially international courts that are based on the concept of universality must fully endorse this ideal in their practice, if they are not to be perceived as hypocritical. Ideally, the courts' aspiration to universality should be based on the conviction that human rights equally apply to all people and that their violation should therefore face sanctions whenever and wherever it occurs. Those who work for more international co-operation for pragmatic reasons – because it serves their interests or contributes to resolving the various global crises (financial system, climate, energy and food) – should also work towards dismantling double standards.

Instead of addressing justified criticism and dismissing unjustified criticism, proponents of international jurisdiction and states and organizations that support it tend to simply ignore this issue in the mistaken belief that a candid examination of its shortcomings would be damaging. Instead of dealing with the charge of double standards in a constructive way, the debate is left entirely in the hands of those who seek to discredit the concept as a whole. The scene is currently dominated by those who resort, with varying degrees of subtlety, to the *tu quoque* objection. Defendants like Milošević and Saddam Hussein are no strangers to using this argument in their defence, if not in court then at least in political public relations battles. The Nuremberg prosecutor Telford Taylor and philosopher Jean-Paul Sartre called for the Nuremberg principles to be applied against those responsible for war crimes in Vietnam, as a standard by which the actions of governments in the future could, if necessary, be assessed in court. In refuting this idea, cynical intellectuals used the occasion of the My Lai massacre as a chance to characterize Nuremberg as a court of exception and a manifestation of victors' justice in an attempt to deny the Nuremberg principles any future application. The impunity for the perpetrators of the My Lai massacre did not represent the "moral deficit of the American people", according to the German lawyer Helmut Quaritsch. Instead, he argues, "it corresponded to the principle according to which nations apportion justice: the distinctions made are political (in a Schmittian sense), that is, states distinguish between friends and foes". He goes on to say that since nations "clearly have a subconscious need to hold friends and foes to different standards, jurisdiction must remain in their own hands".[6] The realists and the Schmittians of this world rejoice in be-

---

6   Helmut Quaritsch, "Epilogue", in Carl Schmitt, *Das internationalrechtliche Verbrechen des Angriffskriegs und der Grundsatz "Nullum crimen, nulla poena sine lege"*, Duncker und Humblot, Berlin, 1994, p. 227 (author's translation).

ing able to repeat over and over again that the idea of law as a universally applicable principle is not viable.

The problem of double standards arose recently in the context of the torture scandals at Abu Ghraib and Guantánamo. No real criminal proceedings have been brought against those responsible for systematic torture; the convictions of a dozen subordinate soldiers represent the extent of the action taken. Western states have been shamefully silent on the matter, whether out of some kind of loyalty to their allies or because they themselves have been complicit in these crimes to a greater (UK) or lesser (Germany) extent. This state of affairs is exploited by influential commentators in the Arab and Muslim world, who are often motivated by factors other than a concern for upholding the prohibition on torture. One need only look to the history of the torture and liquidation centre at Abu Ghraib, one of the most brutal prisons under Saddam Hussein, and the ongoing practice of torture in neighbouring states of Iran, Turkey, Syria and Jordan, to see that hypocrisy is not the preserve of Western states. The examples provided by Abu Ghraib and Guantánamo have discouraging consequences. If, for example, the issue of torture is raised by Western governments, the government pointed at can run the conversation aground by simply pointing to the crimes committed by the USA. Torturers around the world also benefit from the fact that the USA has undermined the absolute prohibition on torture; they now seek to justify their actions by invoking their own state of emergency, their own security concerns and their own fight against terrorists.

10.2. How Selective Is International Criminal Justice?

The preliminary assessment can be summed up as follows. There is no genuine universal international criminal justice, and political horizontal and vertical selectivity abound in this field.

While the tribunals in Nuremberg and Tokyo after the Second World War were established by the victorious Allies, they did not represent 'victors' justice' in the sense that they lacked any of the requirements of a fair trial as was made out by the Nazi defendants and later by the historical revisionists. The trials were in fact quite avant-garde proceedings which laid the normative foundations for a system of international criminal justice.

The *tu quoque* objection made by those on trial in Nuremberg was wholly untenable in light of the sheer enormity of the Nazi crimes. One criticism that may be levelled at the Allies is that, even once a certain period of time had lapsed and a measure of detachment from the Nazi crimes had thus developed, they should have allowed a determination of the legality of specific means and methods of warfare such as the bombing of civilian targets and the use of nuclear weapons, and taken the necessary legal and other measures. The desire of the Western powers and the Soviet Union to keep all means and methods of warfare open was to have dire consequences, with many banned modes of combat still in use long after 1945.

There were no prosecutions for international crimes committed during the colonial wars, partly because nobody was particularly interested in taking criminal action and partly due to the politically rooted inaction that crippled the UN during the Cold War. At the time, there were also practically no human rights organizations active at the international level that might have been in a position to at least report these crimes and to draw attention to them. This changed over the course of the Cold War, as demonstrated by the example of the My Lai massacre.

The tribunals for ex-Yugoslavia and Rwanda showed once again that the ultimate factor at play was political interest and not the desire for global justice or the establishment of a global criminal judiciary. Hence, it should come as no surprise that human rights violations in DR Congo, Turkey and the Philippines, and the grave crimes that had earlier been committed in South and Central America, while to some degree comparable to the crimes that occurred in ex-Yugoslavia and Rwanda, were never the subject of a tribunal and that, as such, double standards were applied.

The tribunals for ex-Yugoslavia and Rwanda and in particular the subsequent hybrid tribunals face much criticism for their perceived selectivity. Using the example of Rwanda, Gerd Hankel demonstrates this very clearly, arguing that group identities often circle around a cultural memory of 'victims and perpetrators', whereby the latter often consider themselves as victims and the 'current' victims as perpetrators. Therefore, the categorical designation of one group as victims, as practised by the Rwanda tribunal, is doomed to failure. Instead, Hankel argues, the cultural memory of the dominating group must acknowledge their own mistakes and admit past wrongs. In the case of Rwanda, the Tutsi must recognize that Hutus were also the victims of grave crimes. He adds, however, that acknowledging injustices on both sides is not the same as finding an equal amount of wrongdoing.[7]

Even before the ICC Statute came into force in 2002, victims and human rights organizations had long turned to national courts, relying on the concept of universal jurisdiction, in the hope of securing individual justice and reparation. In seeking to apply the Pinochet precedent to other powerful perpetrators of international crimes, human rights activists have however faced a number of legal and political defeats.

Not least because of NGO criticism which arose from these organizations' often disappointing experiences during their endeavour to promote international justice, the ICC, the other currently active international and hybrid tribunals, and national courts are increasingly being judged against their own claim to universality. At first glance, it would seem that the ICC fails this test. A closer examination, however, reveals that blame for the Court's universality deficiency cannot be laid entirely at the feet of the Office of the Prosecutor in The Hague. Critics often fail to name concrete situations in which the prosecutor could and should have acted. On the other hand, there have been situations, notably Colombia, in which the prosecution has indeed failed to use its powers to initiate investigations against politically influential suspects.

After 13 years of the ICC, 17 years of practice from national courts in Europe, and 22 years since the establishment of the tribunal for the former Yugoslavia, it remains too soon to draw definite conclusions about this complex area which affects international relations as well as individual nation states. This is even more so if we bear in mind that it took decades before oppressed sections of society, such as the labour and women's movement, were able to make any progress in enforcing their legal demands for equality in national jurisdictions.

Furthermore, a (criminal) justice system should not be declared completely defective just because certain perpetrators, offences or indeed entire forms of criminality may currently enjoy impunity. This is demonstrated by the development of the fight against white-collar crime in the USA and Germany, where up until the last few decades, very few crimi-

---

[7]   Gerd Hankel, "Vergangenheitsaufarbeitung durch die Justiz? – Das Beispiel Ruanda", in Frank Neubacher and Anne Klein (eds.), *Vom Recht der Macht zur Macht des Rechts? Interdisziplinäre Beiträge zur Zukunft internationaler Strafgerichte*, Duncker und Humblot, Berlin, 2006, p. 276.

nal proceedings were ever launched against corporate criminals. Since then, improved investigatory resources, increased action on the part of prosecution authorities and a series of cases and judgments against corruption have led to a remarkable change in the behaviour of large corporations. With this is in mind, international criminal law should be assessed not only in respect of its current state of development but also of its future potential.

10.3. The Solution Offered by Universal Justice

Those involved in the current fight for international and transnational criminal justice for international crimes have highly divergent motivations. This becomes clear if one looks at the mixed coalition that worked on the establishment of an international criminal court at the Rome Conference in 1998, from the 'like-minded' states of the Global North and South, to the UN and other global institutions along with legal experts, academic bodies as well as human rights organizations from the North and social movements from the South. Today, more than 15 years later, one can assume that not all of those involved fully realized what they were creating. Up until the middle of the last decade, the optimistic pronouncements coming in particular from those who work to uphold human rights seemed rather naive. Many states proceeded on the assumption that the ICC would not greatly impinge on their own interests, let alone attempt to bring criminal proceedings against their own activities, a phenomenon the US social scientist Kathryn Sikkink calls "self-entrapment".[8]

The underlying shared interest should, however, remain unchanged: to ensure – in a world of global crises that can increasingly be solved through co-operation only – that minimum standards of human rights are upheld, meaning that crimes against humanity do not occur and that appropriate legal measures are taken where that type of crimes is committed. As has been clear since 11 September 2001 at the latest, this cannot be realized if Western states continue to insist on their own conception of universality thereby ignoring existing double standards. Should this attitude persist, we will see a further decline in the standards that have been eroded over the last years, and all states will have learned from the West's example: respect international legal standards, but only as long as they serve your own interests.

---

[8] Sikkink, 2011, p. 239, see *supra* note 3.

A distinction must, however, be drawn between different Western states. In the last few years, we have witnessed political regression in the USA. If President Obama orders the killing of Osama bin Laden which, as the limited available facts suggest, was carried out in an illegal fashion, and then publicly declares that "justice has been done", we are looking at pre-Nuremberg attitudes. Torture was not used on Nazi leaders, neither during nor after the war, and even those who stood accused of being responsible for millions of murders were never subjected to summary executions. Even more troubling than this defective conception of the law, however, is the ongoing impunity surrounding the torture regime at Guantánamo. Similar – if slightly lesser – accusations are also levelled at the UK in connection with prisoner abuse. Other European countries may rightly be accused of complicity on the basis of their unquestioning cooperation with non-European secret services who partly acquire their information through the use of torture. Criminal proceedings are still ongoing in relation to a number of those international crimes that are actionable in Europe, including in Poland, Italy, Spain and Germany. Those who support the advancement of the global criminal justice project should refrain from attempts to obstruct and derail these proceedings and instead actively support them.

Western states are also engaged in an attempt to shield themselves from accusations that they committed war crimes in the course of humanitarian interventions and during wars undertaken in their fight against terrorism. This manifests itself at various legal and political levels. First of all, the good intentions that may be behind certain interventions mean that they are not characterized as wars of aggression, even if they had been waged in violation of international law.

Secondly, international humanitarian law is too ambiguous to define the legal limits of military action clearly enough to provide adequate protection to civilian populations, particularly in cases of ostensibly 'humanitarian' interventions. Gerd Hankel thus rightly calls for reforms that would protect civilian populations, particularly during air strikes.[9]

Thirdly, weapons such as cluster munitions, cluster bombs and uranium-enriched weapons should be explicitly forbidden. These weapons

---

[9]   Gerd Hankel, *Das Tötungsverbot im Krieg: ein Interventionsversuch*, Hamburger Edition, Hamburg, 2010.

cause long-term damage and are widely considered to violate international law so they should be explicitly proscribed.

Fourthly, Western states evidently want to limit criminal prosecution by international courts to cases of genocide and massacre, to machete wielding Hutus and machine gun toting Serbs, as it were, to the exclusion of war crimes committed by Western states. Even when the use of military force results in massive collateral damage, as happened in Kunduz, those responsible are found to lack the intention of killing civilians. Western parties to the ICC Statute thus benefit from the fact that these war crimes were not committed as part of a plan or policy, or of a large-scale commission of crimes which Article 8 of the ICC Statue requires before the ICC can intervene, but rather as the unintended but widespread side effects of the high technology 'precision' warfare they and their allies preferably resort to. Besides, individual states remain under the discussed obligation to actively pursue investigations in relevant cases.

The fifth and final point, however, is that the required national proceedings frequently are not even initiated, or else are swiftly brought to a close for political reasons.

10.4. The Growing Role of Human Rights Organizations

Many of the positive developments set out in this book would not have come about were it not for social movements, victims' groups and the lawyers and human rights activists working with them. The role of non-state actors is evident if one considers the work done to draw attention to US war crimes in Vietnam through the tribunals of opinion and the anti-war movement, the groundbreaking successes of the Chilean and Argentine human rights movements, and the current global pursuit of justice for human rights violations. These organizations, together with other experts, also exert significant influence on the formulation and interpretation of laws in national, transnational and international forums. Professional and differentiated structures, both local and global, have now emerged that did not exist in 1945, 1960 or even in the 1980s. It should go without saying that the label 'non-governmental' does not necessarily guarantee virtue. Questions of financing, political orientation, instrumentalization by states and sponsors, and the legitimacy of these "entrepreneurs"[10] of international criminal law should of course be borne in mind and followed up.

The involvement of private actors in the discussed criminal proceedings has increased steadily since the 1980s and takes many forms. Some of the functions regularly carried out by human rights organizations include the issuing of early reports about massacres, the filing of complaints with local authorities, the pursuing of legal action through various courts, the conducting of investigations into individual incidents, and the reporting on human rights violations. In addition, a pool of experts has emerged from universities, lawyers' circles, human rights organizations and institutions such as the UN. Professional investigators, particular those working in anthropology and forensics, do essential work in preparing evidence that will stand up to the requirements of criminal procedure. Lawyers determine the legal grounds for filing complaints and take on cases either as members of a public interest group or as representatives of victims and their communities.

10.5. Human Rights Objectives

Over the last two decades, international criminal law has attracted high levels of interest from human rights organizations and sections of the public. Human rights activists are often accused of peddling the politics of morality, relying on moral arguments to appeal to governments and international institutions. Criminal trials of individuals accused of human rights violations also tend to capture the imagination of non-state actors. They receive more societal plaudits for stepping in on what is demonstrably the side of 'good', for the victims, and against the 'bad guys', as opposed to championing some more complex vision of a better society that might be difficult to achieve. They can participate in the exercise of state power, sometimes even direct its course, and join in the chorus of those welcoming the conviction of a perpetrator. Assuming that it is conducted in a politically aware manner, this approach can be a pragmatic one, with an eye to utopian potential, if recourse is had to legal proceedings in order to pursue some further-reaching aims in the interest of the marginalized who are most frequently located in the Global South. On the other hand, there is an element of inherent danger in calling on powerful states and

---

[10] Frédéric Mégret, "Three Dangers for the International Criminal Court: A Critical Look at a Consensual Project", in *Finnish Yearbook of International Law*, 2001, vol. 12, p. 242.

governments to initiate criminal proceedings and to support these, if trials are only carried out if and to the extent that they serve the interests of the powerful.

As valuable as the various efforts of human rights organizations may be to individual legal proceedings, and as important as they may be as psychological and material support for those affected, there is a further important consideration. All of these activities must be assessed in terms of whether they are genuinely suited to bringing about change in the situation at hand and whether, in doing so, they serve long-term strategies and objectives. As such, there is a need within the area of international criminal law for a more forward-looking human rights policy that is aimed at social and political change.

Universalizing the existing practice of global criminal justice cannot be achieved without engaging with the current political reality. This reality is determined by the political framework in which powerful actors, such as the veto powers, states and regional elites, pursue their own political interests. Yet the power relations within this political field are not set in stone; non-state actors and social movements have a substantial role to play in the struggle for the law and political influence. Crucially, an imagined overly strict separation between the spheres of law and politics which is championed by many advocates will not solve the problem posed by political interests.

Instead, the debate on the pros and cons of international criminal justice and its repercussions must turn its focus to the affected communities. In this context, it is important to work together with other disciplines and in particular with the victims of human rights violations and their communities themselves. By assessing concrete situations in respect of the consequences of prevailing impunity for past crimes, the need for some process of coming to terms with past events, becomes evident. However, such processes do not necessarily have to comprise criminal proceedings. Where they *have* included criminal trials, the repercussions of these proceedings need to be thoroughly examined. In this respect, it is not enough to simply catalogue the existence or non-existence of criminal charges, trials and convictions. Instead, a closer look into the impact of these proceedings within the different discourses of the affected communities is called for.

What we need, therefore, is an international criminal justice policy with a human rights content.[11] This policy should resort to the language and logic of law while recognizing the limits of legal and criminal law efforts. It has to aim at influencing the political discourse and it must also allow the resort to the instruments of political struggle. In the formative years of international criminal law, prominent figures such as Judge Garzón were helpful and indeed vital in challenging traditional ideas, and processes. Their work helped the European judiciary to become accustomed to the idea that they could get involved in cases such as the crimes of the Argentine military dictatorship in the 1970s or the massacre at Srebrenica. These important individuals have demonstrated good sense for the feasibility of these kinds of cases, bearing in mind the interest of the victims. With a powerful combination of naivety, wilful ignorance of existing political circumstances, and a vision of genuine universal justice, these figures managed to forge some scope for progress which now needs to be exploited as sensibly as possible. There is no doubt about the need for support, legal and otherwise, for all victims of international crimes. But while the use of attention-grabbing buzzwords and symbolism may have worked well over the past 20 years, all parties have now learned to adapt to the use of these tools with the result that much of their impact is lost. Due to the still limited legal avenues available, it is highly recommendable to strategically select the avenue to pursue human rights litigation in the light of the circumstances of each case. Consultations with the relevant local actors are crucial to identify the approach which is most likely to bring about a positive impact in the affected communities.

Consequently, and in light of the significant limits of international prosecutions and particularly the ICC, more emphasis should in the future be placed on proceedings before national courts. From the perspective of victims and human rights organizations, national legal systems do not offer the prominent platform afforded by trials in The Hague. Yet the national framework frequently offers more possible intervention points and the chance to advance the aim of comprehensive accountability for grave human rights violations on a step-by-step basis. By this measure, the European criminal proceedings as to Chilean and Argentine crimes were a success because of the impact they had on both the national judiciaries

---

[11] On this, see Andreas Fischer-Lescano and Philip Liste, "Völkerrechtspolitik: Zu Trennung und Verknüpfung von Politik und Recht der Weltgesellschaft", in *Zeitschrift für International Beziehungen*, 2005, vol. 12, no. 2, pp. 209–249.

and societies. Attempts to emulate these cases, however, have led to a number of setbacks – there are now a number of new obstacles to universal jurisdiction proceedings that did not exist just a few years ago. The same applies to the civil suits in the USA mentioned earlier, which were often directed more at the American public or the American justice system and thus lost sight of the real objective. This kind of isolated – or at best loosely connected – activities made it very easy for the respondents and their political allies to fend off the attempts to hold them accountable in court. With this in mind, human rights and development organizations as well as academic institutions seeking to address international crimes are now making a strategic effort to carefully choose the instrument to resort to in every case in the light of the potential impact of the chosen approach, including beyond the individual case.

The success of transnational criminal justice should not be measured solely by reference to the (provisional) results to date such as the launching of formal investigation, or the number of formal indictments and convictions handed down. On no account should the length of a sentence be seen as a measure of success, even if victims of human rights violations and their family members often feel differently. In assessing litigation results, it is crucial to differentiate between different relevant dimensions, such as the formal initiation of legal proceedings, the clarification of the facts of a case, the adoption of a judgment or a decision by a court or another body such as a truth commission, and the handing down and execution of a sentence. In some cases, certain results might best be achieved through the use of legal instruments other than criminal law, such as compensation claims or complaints against states with regional courts or UN bodies. Even defeats in court can ultimately turn out to benefit a cause in the medium to long term.

At the end of all these considerations and activities, there must remain one minimum goal: to ensure that the Sri Lankan diplomat quoted at the start of this book who claimed that "winners are never tried for war crimes" and all those responsible for war crimes in Sri Lanka meet the same fate as the Argentine military junta. The Argentine former military commander, the now deceased General Roberto Viola, declared during his inaugural visit to the USA in 1981 that "a victorious army is not investigated".[12] Today, Viola's surviving military colleagues week after week find themselves in the dock before Argentine courts.

But it will not be possible to speak of a universal criminal justice system with equal rights and access to justice for all until the instigators and organizers of Guantánamo and other atrocities in Chechnya are held accountable for their actions. While criminal proceedings might be concerned primarily with holding individuals to account, they can also, if used in the right way, represent the first step in a comprehensive process of coming to terms with past crimes in a way that facilitates the restoration of peace in the affected communities. Uncovering the causes of past crimes can then serve to deepen our understanding, ultimately leaving us better equipped to prevent the occurrence of atrocities in the future.

---

[12]   Quoted by Sikkink, 2011, p. 9, see *supra* note 3.

INDEX

A

Abd-Al-Rahman, Ali Muhammad Ali 94
Abu Ghraib 69, 70, 82, 112
Adenauer, Konrad 20
Africa 3, 27, 67, 68, 103, 105
African Commission on Human Rights 97
African Court on Human Rights 97
African Union 53, 67
Agent Orange 35, 42
Akayesu decision 54
Akayesu, Jean Paul 52
al-Bashir, Omar Hassan 94
Albright, Madeleine 46
al-Gaddafi, Muammar 1, 98
Algerian independence movement 62
Algerian War 29
Alien Tort Claims Act 63, 86
Alleg, Henri 30
Almatov, Zokirjon 81
Al-Senussi, Abdullah 97
Amnesty International 48, 66, 69, 97
anti-colonial liberation movements 27
Arab Spring 97
Arbour, Louise 47
Arendt, Hannah 107
Argentina 62, 63, 65, 66, 73, 75, 80, 87, 109, 120, 121
Armenian genocide 40
Asia-Pacific War 41
Aussaresses, Paul 31
Austria 69

B

Ba'ath Party 57
Balkan wars 53
Bangladesh 45
Barbie, Klaus 30
Basso, Lelio 40
Battle of Algiers 30
Bauer, Fritz 22

Belgium 27, 33, 64, 67, 69, 76
Bemba, Jean-Pierre 96
Benchellali, Mourad 72
Ben-Gurion, David 107
Bensouda, Fatou 95
Biafra 45
Biddle, Francis 14
bin Laden, Osama 116
Blé Goudé, Charles 97
Bouhired, Djamila 30
Bowman, Herbert D. 56
Bozizé, François 96
Brammertz, Serge 51
Buckel, Sonja 41
Bush administration 3, 70
Bush, George W. 72, 90
Bussi, Antonio Domingo 64

C

Calley, William 36, 37
Cambodia 6, 35, 56
Castresana, Carlos 64
Čelebići prison camp 55
Center for Constitutional Rights 62, 70, 72
Central African Republic 95
Chad 67–69
Chea, Nuan 57
Chechnya 68
Cheney, Dick 71
Chile 62, 63, 65, 66, 73, 75
China 17, 74
Chirac, Jacques 58
Chui, Mathieu Ngudjolo 91
CIA 36, 71, 72
Clinton, Bill 90
Cold War 2, 11, 20, 29, 35, 43, 113
Colombia 99–101, 114
Colonia Dignidad 80
colonial crimes 26, 27, 31, 32, 77
colonial wars 25–33
comfort women 17, 41

K

L

M

N

Nagasaki 18
national courts *See* domestic courts
NATO 16, 42, 47, 48, 49, 51, 98
NATO crimes 49, 50
Nazi crimes 7, 18, 21, 22, 78, 79, 113
Nazi party 12, 19
Nazi trials 21–24
Ndumbe III, Kum'a 8, 31
Netherlands 27, 28, 32, 86
Nicaragua 40
Nimitz, Chester 14
Nixon administration 37
non-state actors 62, 85, 117, 118, 119
nulla poena sine lege 13
Nuremberg Military Tribunal 11
Nuremberg principles 23, 40, 111
Nuremberg trials 2, 5, 11, 14, 18, 19, 23,
    26, 112
Nyamwisi, Mbusa 92

O

Obama, Barack 71, 116
Odhiambo, Okot 93
Ogoni people 86
Omar, Abu 71
Ongwen, Dominic 93
Operation Storm 51
Otti, Vincent 93

P

Pakistan 26, 83
Pal, Radhabinod 18
Palestine 90, 104, 105
Papua New Guinea 86
Peer, William 37
Permanent Peoples' Tribunal 40
Peru 62
Philippines 45
Phoenix Program 36
Pinochet case 2
Pinochet, Augusto 3, 65, 66
Politbüro 80
Politbüro case 79
Portugal 27
post-colonial theories 25

private actors *See* non-state actors
privilegium odiosum 12
Public Interest Lawyers 102

Q

Quaritsch, Helmut 111
Quattara, Alassane 97

R

Rasse- und Siedlungshauptamt trial 15
Rawagede 32
Realpolitik 1, 4
Red Army 19
Responsibility to Protect 48
right of self-determination of peoples 32,
    40, 44
right to development 44
Rio Tinto 86
Röchling 85
Roxin, Claus 79
Rumsfeld, Donald 69, 71, 72, 82
Russel Tribunal 40
Russell, Bertrand 40
Russia 68, 69
Ruto, William 96
Rwabukombe, Onesphore 82
Rwanda 43, 45, 52, 82, 92, 113

S

Samphan, Khieu 57
Sang, Joshua Arap 96
Santoyo, Mauricio 101
Saro Wiwa, Ken 86
Sartre, Jean-Paul 40, 111
Sassi, Nizar 72
Schabas, William 18
Schmitt, Carl 4, 14, 85
Scilingo, Adolfo 65
Second World War 8, 18
selectivity, horizontal 7, 59, 93
selectivity, political 48, 104, 105
selectivity, vertical 7, 17, 59, 93
Senegal 67
Serbia 16, 47, 49, 78
Sheehan, Neil 38
Shell 86

T

V

W

Y

U

TOAEP TEAM

OTHER VOLUMES IN THE
FICHL PUBLICATION SERIES

Morten Bergsmo, Mads Harlem and Nobuo Hayashi (editors):
Importing Core International Crimes into National Law
Torkel Opsahl Academic EPublisher
Oslo, 2010
FICHL Publication Series No. 1 (Second Edition, 2010)
ISBN 978-82-93081-00-5

Nobuo Hayashi (editor):
National Military Manuals on the Law of Armed Conflict
Torkel Opsahl Academic EPublisher
Oslo, 2010
FICHL Publication Series No. 2 (Second Edition, 2010)
ISBN 978-82-93081-02-9

Morten Bergsmo, Kjetil Helvig, Ilia Utmelidze and Gorana Žagovec:
The Backlog of Core International Crimes Case Files in Bosnia and Herzegovina
Torkel Opsahl Academic EPublisher
Oslo, 2010
FICHL Publication Series No. 3 (Second Edition, 2010)
ISBN 978-82-93081-04-3

Morten Bergsmo (editor):
Criteria for Prioritizing and Selecting Core International Crimes Cases
Torkel Opsahl Academic EPublisher
Oslo, 2010
FICHL Publication Series No. 4 (Second Edition, 2010)
ISBN 978-82-93081-06-7

Morten Bergsmo and Pablo Kalmanovitz (editors):
Law in Peace Negotiations
Torkel Opsahl Academic EPublisher
Oslo, 2010
FICHL Publication Series No. 5 (Second Edition, 2010)
ISBN 978-82-93081-08-1

Morten Bergsmo, César Rodríguez Garavito, Pablo Kalmanovitz and Maria Paula Saffon (editors):
Distributive Justice in Transitions
Torkel Opsahl Academic EPublisher
Oslo, 2010
FICHL Publication Series No. 6 (2010)
ISBN 978-82-93081-12-8

Morten Bergsmo (editor):
Complementarity and the Exercise of Universal Jurisdiction for Core International Crimes
Torkel Opsahl Academic EPublisher
Oslo, 2010
FICHL Publication Series No. 7 (2010)
ISBN 978-82-93081-14-2

Morten Bergsmo (editor):
Active Complementarity: Legal Information Transfer
Torkel Opsahl Academic EPublisher
Oslo, 2011
FICHL Publication Series No. 8 (2011)
ISBN 978-82-93081-55-5 (PDF)
ISBN 978-82-93081-56-2 (print)

Sam Muller, Stavros Zouridis, Morly Frishman and Laura Kistemaker (editors):
The Law of the Future and the Future of Law
Torkel Opsahl Academic EPublisher
Oslo, 2010
FICHL Publication Series No. 11 (2011)
ISBN 978-82-93081-27-2

Morten Bergsmo, Alf Butenschøn Skre and Elisabeth J. Wood (editors):
Understanding and Proving International Sex Crimes
Torkel Opsahl Academic EPublisher
Beijing, 2012
FICHL Publication Series No. 12 (2012)
ISBN 978-82-93081-29-6

Morten Bergsmo (editor):
Thematic Prosecution of International Sex Crimes
Torkel Opsahl Academic EPublisher
Beijing, 2012
FICHL Publication Series No. 13 (2012)

ISBN 978-82-93081-31-9

Terje Einarsen:
The Concept of Universal Crimes in International Law
Torkel Opsahl Academic EPublisher
Oslo, 2012
FICHL Publication Series No. 14 (2012)
ISBN 978-82-93081-33-3

莫滕·伯格斯默 凌岩 （主编）：
国家主权与国际刑法
Torkel Opsahl Academic EPublisher
Beijing, 2012
FICHL Publication Series No. 15 (2012)
ISBN 978-82-93081-58-6

Morten Bergsmo and LING Yan (editors):
State Sovereignty and International Criminal Law
Torkel Opsahl Academic EPublisher
Beijing, 2012
FICHL Publication Series No. 15 (2012)
ISBN 978-82-93081-35-7

Morten Bergsmo and CHEAH Wui Ling (editors):
Old Evidence and Core International Crimes
Torkel Opsahl Academic EPublisher
Beijing, 2012
FICHL Publication Series No. 16 (2012)
ISBN 978-82-93081-60-9

YI Ping:
戦争と平和の間——発足期日本国際法学における「正しい戦争」
の観念とその帰結
Torkel Opsahl Academic EPublisher
Beijing, 2013
FICHL Publication Series No. 17 (2013)
ISBN 978-82-93081-66-1

Morten Bergsmo and SONG Tianying (editors):
On the Proposed Crimes Against Humanity Convention
Torkel Opsahl Academic EPublisher
Brussels, 2014
FICHL Publication Series No. 18 (2014)

ISBN 978-82-93081-96-8

Morten Bergsmo (editor):
Quality Control in Fact-Finding
Torkel Opsahl Academic EPublisher
Florence, 2013
FICHL Publication Series No. 19 (2013)
ISBN 978-82-93081-78-4

Morten Bergsmo, CHEAH Wui Ling and YI Ping (editors):
Historical Origins of International Criminal Law: Volume 1
Torkel Opsahl Academic EPublisher
Brussels, 2014
FICHL Publication Series No. 20 (2014)
ISBN 978-82-93081-11-1

Morten Bergsmo, CHEAH Wui Ling and YI Ping (editors):
Historical Origins of International Criminal Law: Volume 2
Torkel Opsahl Academic EPublisher
Brussels, 2014
FICHL Publication Series No. 21 (2014)
ISBN 978-82-93081-13-5

All volumes are freely available online at http://www.fichl.org/publication-series/. Printed copies may be ordered from distributors indicated at http://www.fichl.org/torkel-opsahl-academic-epublisher/distribution/, including from http://www.amazon.co.uk/. For reviews of earlier books in this Series in academic journals, please see http://www.fichl.org/torkel-opsahl-academic-epublisher/reviews-of-toaep-books/.